Heartfulness

The history of your happiness is the

history of your feeling connected.

Vironika Tugaleva, *The Love Mindset*

First published 2016

Exisle Publishing Pty Ltd
'Moonrising', Narone Creek Road, Wollombi, NSW 2325, Australia
P.O. Box 60–490, Titirangi, Auckland 0642, New Zealand
www.exislepublishing.com

A CiP record for this book is available from the National Library of
Australia

ISBN 978-1-925335-00-2

Design and typesetting by Big Cat Design
Typeset in Minion Pro 10.5 on 14.5pt
Printed in China

This book uses paper sourced under ISO 14001 guidelines from well-
managed forests and other controlled sources.

10 9 8 7 6 5 4 3 2 1

Disclaimer

HeartfuLness

Beyond Mindfulness, Finding Your Real Life

DR STEPHEN McKENZIE

EXISLE PUBLISHING

CONTENTS

PART 1

DISCOVERING HEARTFULNESS, AND WHY IT IS WORTH DISCOVERING

part 2

paths to heartfulness

part 3

new heartful horizons

DISCOVERING HEARTFULNESS, AND WHY IT IS WORTH DISCOVERING

CHAPTER 1

Find your heartfulness-opening potential

Great problems allow great solutions.

Are you as happy as you can be?

Do you have as much peace of mind as you can have?

Do you have as much peace of heart as you can have?

Do you realize the vital connection between your mind
and your heart?

Are you fully alive?

If you answered 'yes' to the above questions, congratulations. Please keep reading, because this book will help you help other people to be really aware, really connected, really human, really alive and really happy.

If you answered 'no' to the above questions, congratulations, you have a wonderful opportunity to live more fully, deeply and happily, by realising what is getting in your way. Please keep reading, because this book will help you remember your connection with the source of your happiness, health, awareness, acceptance, love and life.

This book is for you, no matter who you are, or who you think you are.

This book will help you be really aware, really connected, really human, really alive and really happy.

We don't have to learn about light, or understand it or believe in it, to experience it and to benefit from it. We don't have to learn about heartfulness, or understand it or believe in it, to experience it and to benefit from it — we only have to *allow* it. Being heartful simply means being fully connected — with ourselves and with other people — and therefore fully alive.

Heartfulness isn't just for people who believe in it, or for people who believe in anything. Heartfulness is for *all* people, no matter what they believe. Heartfulness gives us all a way out — of our mind-made disconnections and stresses; and a way in — to our natural flow of connectedness, peace and happiness. Reconnecting with who we really are, together, is the greatest journey we can make, so let's begin.

Heartfulness-opening Potential Test

Before we start on our journey home to heartfulness, you are invited to take this heartfulness-opening potential test (HOP), because it can help you find out what you need to know about yourself and about other people.

Answer each of the following nine questions on a scale from
1 — Not at all, to **10 — Totally**

The more honest you are, the more valid the test.

1. How kind are you?

1   2   3   4   5   6   7   8   9   10

2. How well do you respond to adversity?

1   2   3   4   5   6   7   8   9   10

3. How good-humoured are you?

1   2   3   4   5   6   7   8   9   10

4. How content are you?

1   2   3   4   5   6   7   8   9   10

5. How loving are you?

1   2   3   4   5   6   7   8   9   10

6. How courageous are you?

1   2   3   4   5   6   7   8   9   10

7. How knowledgeable are you?

1   2   3   4   5   6   7   8   9   10

8. How hopeful are you?

1　2　3　4　5　6　7　8　9　10

9. How creative are you?

1　2　3　4　5　6　7　8　9　10

Calculate your Heartfulness-opening Potential

HOP Step 1: Add up the points that you scored out of 10 for each question.
HOP Step 2: Subtract your added-up score from 90.

The higher your HOP score, the greater your potential to open your heartfulness. You can take this test again after reading this book to discover whether anything has changed.

CHAPTER 2

Home is where the heartfulness is

In Asian languages, the word for 'mind' and the word for 'heart' are the same word … So when you hear the word 'mindfulness', if you're not in some sense automatically hearing the word 'heartfulness' you're misunderstanding it. And mindfulness in any event is not a concept; it's a way of being. And it's a way of being awake.

Dr Jon Kabat-Zinn — interview with Krista Tippett

What have we progressed to?
What have we gained?
What have we lost?
Why did we lose it?
How can we get it back?

There are many wonderful and inspiring stories about people desperately searching everywhere for something important that they think they have lost, and then finally finding it at home. These include stories of discovery and creativity, and healing and hope, and they can be our stories. Our stories naturally end happily when we remember our way home — to our source, our centre, our essence, our heart. Heartfulness is our way home.

A small story

There was a time when I didn't have enough time, or thought I didn't. There was a time when I was a commuter and spent my time saving time; I still don't know why. I was a member of the time herd, charging every morning and evening up stairs and escalators that led from darkness to light, and from light to darkness.

In the mornings we charged up from a subterranean station and mind-set into the light of another working day. We were all going in the same direction except for a short man who looked tall as he stood facing us at the entrance to the light, as we arrived for yet another working day. He was homeless yet not workless, his job was selling us The Big Issue, *a fortnightly publication that helps the homeless afford homes and gives us a new way of looking at life.*

'Welcome, all you miserable-looking people, to the outside world!'

One time, as I engaged in a Grand Prix passing manoeuvre that saved me yet another sad second, it struck me that we can change perspectives as easily as we can change clothes or moods or gears.

There was a time when we were timeless. How can we re-discover what it 'is like to join the human race, and stop trying to win it?

Coming home

> We shall not cease from exploration
> And the end of all our exploring
> Will be to arrive where we started
> And know the place for the first time.
>
> *TS Eliot*, 'Little Gidding'

How long has it been since someone asked you if you are happy? Maybe someone asked you if you are keeping busy, or if you are stressed, or even if you share the same stress as everyone else seems to have. But none of these is the same as being happy.

We have progressed a long way since we left our caves, and before that our trees, our oceans, and our universal oneness — but how far have we come? It is true that we live longer now on average than we used to, and most of us are happy enough to be alive for as long as we can be, or at least consider it a better bet than its alternative. But are we really happy?

Are we really happy with our progressively more powerful drugs and therapies and technologies, when we also have progressively higher rates of addiction, pollution, stress, suicide, anxiety, depression, insomnia and general undiagnosed misery?

What price have we paid for our technical progress? What diabolical deal have we done? Most of us have more material wealth now than our predecessors had, but do we have more life richness? Most of us have gizmos that allow us to talk to people a long way away from us, but can we talk to the person sitting in the next train seat or workstation? Most of us are megabyte millionaires, but are we rich in experience? We can access innumerable websites and apps, but are we really *connected*?

Lost paradises and diabolical deals are not recent inventions. The English poet Milton famously wrote about *Paradise Lost* and much less famously about *Paradise Regained* in the seventeenth century. The German dramatist Goethe famously wrote about someone selling his soul in *Dr Faustus* in the nineteenth century. Stories about our falling from divine grace or doing a sucker's deal or losing our way home or stuffing up our lives are as old as Adam and Eve, and even older. There is a Greek myth about an ancient Greek god called

Prometheus who gave us fire, symbolising thought, after which Zeus, the leader of the gods, punished him severely for giving us this mixed blessing.

About 2500 years ago, great life teachers emerged at about the same time in northern India (Gautama the Buddha), China (Lao Tzu) and ancient Greece (Socrates and Plato). This proliferation of practical human help probably wasn't random, it probably happened because cities were emerging, and with them the stresses and disconnections that this 'progress' from our traditional life has caused. We have been stressed for a long time by the emergence of cities, and quite possibly well before that by the emergence of other major lifestyle changes. However, our great modern problem isn't that we have lost our natural paradise, but that we have forgotten where to find it.

Before we can find the lost paradise of our full human potential, however, we need to solve the great cosmic whodunit mystery. Why did we lose what's most important to us? This is the human equivalent to the great dinosaur disappearance whodunit, and solving it is vitally important to our happiness and health. Fortunately, some clues have been discovered by our great human help systems, otherwise known as our great philosophies and religions. These practical and powerful life manuals have had their vital ingredients extracted and re-branded, and been sold back to us as modern panaceas, such as cognitive behavioural therapy (CBT). Indeed, CBT was described by Marcus Aurelius about 2000 years before it was 'invented':

> *If you are distressed by anything external, the pain is not due to the thing itself, but to your estimate of it; and this you have the power to revoke at any moment.*

Mindfulness is another popular modern re-branding of an eternal truth, described in *Mindfulness for Life*[1] as an 'overnight lifestyle and clinical sensation that is thousands of years old'.

Extracting modern meaning from ancient knowledge systems has caused us huge problems that we are only now beginning to realize, such as the collective loss of our meaningful living context, or *heart*. All of these ancient knowledge systems tell us things that are remarkably simple, so simple that they can get lost in their translations into complicated theories and self-help strategies. What makes us happy, or rather what *allows* us to be happy, is simple connection with other people. What

makes us unhappy is … disconnection. We lose heart and heartfulness when we lose our connection with who we really are, together, in who we think we are, alone.

All roads lead to home, eventually …

Where Thou Art, That is Home.
Emily Dickinson, 'Where Thou Art, That Is Home'

Don't worry if you don't know what's wrong with your life, and don't worry if you do. Don't even worry if you're worried — that's just what our minds do because it's their job, they are worry factories.

We can regain the paradise of living in our heartland. How? How do we trade back up to what we have cheated ourselves out of? How can we be truly happy, fulfilled, at peace and also genuinely productive, when we are living in a time when religions are old, philosophy is sick, families are unfashionable, medicine has lost heart, God is misunderstood, psychiatry is going mad, law is losing its appeal, science is losing its magic, and Oprah has retired … ? What do we do next?

There is a way into suffering and there is a way out of it. And the way out is in the last place that we would think to look for it, because our way out is actually our way in, to our human heart.

Our way home — nine paths to heartfulness

When we are heartful, we are fully alive and living in light, lightness and delight. There are nine paths to heartfulness, which we will now explore:

- **kindness**
- **adversity**
- **humour**
- **contentment**
- **love**
- **courage**
- **knowledge**
- **hope**
- **creativity.**

We can't *become* heartful because we *already are* heartful. Realising our natural heartfulness — our connectedness — lets us live in this infinite loving space rather than in our mind-made neurotic claustrophobia. Heartfulness gives us a brave new world of opportunities to live life as it really is, rather than keeping *wanting to live it* as something else. It might seem as if we are hanging onto so much baggage in our bodies, minds and hearts that we can never let it go; however, our heaviest baggage is actually the easiest to let go, once we realize that it's just baggage.

It doesn't matter which of the nine paths to heartfulness we follow, because all heartful paths lead to home, when we stay on them.

A small story

I was once walking down a mountain in Dharakot in India with a friend. I had just bought a book at an ancient monastery that I was very much looking forward to reading. Out of nowhere, a group of monkeys appeared in the forest in front of us, and this gave me such a fright that I dropped the book. One of the monkeys grabbed the book and ran off into the forest with it. I gave chase. Suddenly the monkey with the book stopped running, and a very big monkey next to it bared its very large teeth at me. I looked at the now large group of monkeys, and they looked at me. I was paralysed with fear and indecision. In that moment, Kylie's voice connected with me from down the mountain: 'Let it go, Doc, just let it go!'

I realized that, despite my attachment, all that I had lost was an object, and I walked away. Maybe the monkey responded to the same voice, because it dropped the book and left with the other monkeys. I picked up the book and went home. I don't remember what the book purported to be about, however I now realize what it was really about — heartfulness.

We all have a story about losing something that we think is valuable, and then realising that we didn't lose anything valuable at all, because what's of real value is always where it always was — in our hearts.

Another small story

*I was about 30 years old when I learned that I had lost something that
I hadn't previously realized the real value of: a friend from my youth.
Although I had not seen him in years, he had once been a big part of my
life and he still meant a lot to me. That he was gone, and so young, was a
huge loss, even though he had played no part in my daily life for so long.
My mind stampeded against its barriers because it couldn't accept that what
had happened had happened.*

*However, after frantically searching through my mind for what I
thought I had lost, I realized that I could never find what I was really
looking for there. When I stopped searching I allowed a real discovery —
that love is never lost. My friend would always live on in my heart.*

The bottomless line

Our human story is a story of hope. Our great problems can force our great
solutions when we open our eyes and see, and open our minds and understand, and open our hearts and love.

References and further reading

1   McKenzie, S and Hassed, C. (2012). *Mindfulness for Life.* Exisle, Wollombi.
2   McKenzie, S. (2013). *Mindfulness at Work.* Exisle, Wollombi.

CHAPTER 3

Connecting heart and mindfulness

There is much more to being mindful than just being in the present moment. You have to be in the present moment with a clear mind, and a mind that is in assessment mode, and that's when the wise advocate part of the mind makes it much more of a genuine mindfulness, because mindfulness in the genuine tradition has always been the guardian of the mind ... against false thoughts and distracting impulse. You need the assessment aspect, that's very important. Just being in the present with distracting impulses, that's not enough! What they call mindfulness wouldn't work over the long term in such an adulterated form.

Dr Jeffrey Schwartz — from an interview with the author on Life, what's in it for me?
94.7 The Pulse FM, December 2014

Can we insult someone mindfully?

Can we commit a crime mindfully?

Can we even commit murder mindfully?

If we direct our awareness to our bad actions, really feel the sensations in our body as we commit them, and fully accept them, is this mindfulness? There is more to mindfulness than directing our awareness, being fully aware of the present moment as experienced via our bodily sensations, and accepting what we are aware of. True mindfulness occurs in a broad human context of:

- **our connection with other people and our deep level of being, which naturally connects us with other people, and**
- **the human help systems, or belief systems, that give us the whole of mindfulness, not just the bits of it that we have extracted because they seem to help us most and fastest.**

One of the great human help traditions from which mindfulness has emerged is Buddhism. The essence of mindfulness has also been described in Christianity and in many other human help systems. One of the Asian words that the great mindfulness/heartfulness researcher and popularizer Dr Jon Kabat Zin said could be translated as heartfulness, as well as mindfulness, is *sati*, which is from Gautama the Buddha's language, Pali. This word has been translated as 'awareness', and is described as the spiritual, psychological or essential human capacity we need in order to be enlightened.

According to Buddhism, it is not enough just to have *sati*, which has recently reincarnated into modern techniques such as acceptance therapy. Instead, we need 'correct' *sati* or '*sammā-sati*'. This broadens mindfulness from its modern and increasingly limited manifestation, and links it with morality (*sila*) and wisdom (*panya*). Deep life wisdom includes the vital understanding that *all things pass* at a surface level, and also *never pass* at a deeper, essential, eternal level.

So while we can commit crimes mindfully according to the adulterated meaning of the term, we can't according to the original meaning — we can't commit crimes or other harmful actions *heartfully*.

The heart of the mindfulness matter

*Your vision will become clear only when you look
into your heart. Who looks outside, dreams; who
looks inside, awakens.*

Carl Jung

Mindfulness has become extremely popular. This is because it is the natural antidote to the damaging side-effects of a modern world, which is progressing rapidly towards more communal stress and less community. Mindfulness helps us live our lives happily, peacefully and productively, and it can help us prevent, manage and heal many of our psychological and physical problems. Mindfulness helps us *be* without requiring us to be anything in particular, or to believe anything in particular. We don't need to have faith in mindfulness for it to work — at work, at home and at play — and we don't need to join a particular organisation or belief system to practise it and benefit from it. Mindfulness can almost be seen as a universal panacea. It is:

- free as well as freeing,
- anyone can practise it, and
- it has no side effects.

So why then aren't we all mindful? To answer this question we need to look at what mindfulness includes and doesn't include, and we need to look at the relationship between our minds and our hearts. The reason why the ancient words for the mind and the heart were the same is that these were once seen as totally connected, just as *we* were once seen as totally connected.

Mindfulness isn't a recent invention, despite its recent popularity. It's actually not any kind of invention, because it is our natural state, and it was given to us to discover or actually re-discover by ancient traditions. Mindfulness is typically presented as a technique that will help us achieve highly useful outcomes such as increased health and happiness and productivity; however, it is really much more than this.

Mindfulness the word and mindfulness the product are not mindfulness the essence, just as our name and our jobs aren't our essence. Many people who have turned to what they think mindfulness offers are now looking for new self-help toys, because we want more than a technique, no matter how useful. What we really want is something that is complete, and true, and therefore eternal, so that we will never lose its benefits. Therefore, mindfulness needs to evolve back to its original state to reach its full potential, so that it can help us evolve back to *our* original state to reach our full potential.

Some modern mindfulness maladies

Problems with the modern iteration of mindfulness include its:

- *Name:* The word 'mindfulness' means the opposite of what mindfulness really is. Being mindful means having a clear, undistracted and open mind, not a full one. 'Mindlessness' is actually closer to what 'mindfulness' really means.

- *Packaging:* In the interests of universality, or rather in the interests of appealing to everyone, or of not offending anyone, mindfulness has been packaged as a stand-alone technique. However, it is really a living component of the great human help systems that it came from.

- *Lack of connectedness:* Mindfulness the self-help technique doesn't get to the essence or heart of what is really wrong with us, and what can and will be really right with us. Mindfulness the self-help technique does not fully connect us with other people or with ourselves.

- *Emphasis on 'mind' rather than on 'full':* Mindfulness has come to mean being mindful of our minds, and occasionally our bodies, and we have forgotten our hearts. This means that we have forgotten the deep connections that make mindfulness and life real. Mindfulness in its modern Western manifestation matches our obsession with our minds.

We have also attached meditation to our obsession with our minds and with

'de-stressing' them. This often means actively and exhaustingly sorting ourselves out, trying to make our thoughts better than they are, rather than just resting in awareness and acceptance of our passing thought parade. This is why so many of us still need the living traditions and examples of wise men and women from the East, who brought with them much more than gold, frankincense and myrrh. Connecting with our heart and our home has never gone out of fashion in the heartful homelands.

In short, modern mindfulness has lost heart.

Taking heartfulness

> If someone comes along and shoots an arrow into your
> heart, it's fruitless to stand there and yell at the person. It
> would be much better to turn your attention to the fact that
> there's an arrow in your heart …
>
> *Pema Chödrön,* Start Where You Are: A Guide to Compassionate Living

We can link words like 'mind' and 'heart' and even 'soul', which the ancient Greeks called *psyche* (the origin of the word 'psychology', the study of the mind) and what these words are meant to describe. We can do this by peeling away what we *think* they mean until all we have left is what we *know* they mean: our experience of them. When we do this we are on a fantastic journey to the centre of our being, and we will eventually arrive at the heart of our matter. Heartfulness is a word that links with other key human words and describes what it truly and deeply and essentially is to be human.

Heartfulness is our missing link between our great and greatly misunderstood life knowledge systems, such as psychology, philosophy and religion. It is also our missing link between self-help and self-discovery.

Heartfulness is our living connection with:

- **psychology's (Abraham Maslow's)** *self-actualisation* **— we are happy when we are living our life to our full potential**

- Buddhism's essential teaching that we are all enlightened, when we wake up to our real selves
- Christianity's essential teaching that the Kingdom of Heaven is within
- Vedantic philosophy's essential teaching that we are 'not two'
- yoga's connection between mind, body and spirit
- Lao Tzu's going with the flow
- Socrates' 'I know nothing', and even, much more recently, Paul Newman as Cool Hand Luke's 'sometimes nothing is a real cool hand!', and
- mindfulness's non-judgemental awareness and acceptance of our bodily sensations — with heartfulness we can also be non-judgementally aware and accepting of our emotions and their reasons, which can result in sensation storms that can blow us away, if we don't know what they are.

The bottomless line

At the heart of our living matter is space — nothingness. Pure consciousness. This turns into our mind and then our brain and then our behaviours, and is Shakespeare's 'stuff that dreams are made on'. To be heartful is to live life from its core, from its deep essence that connects all of us and allows us to be, and to be happy, fulfilled and free, together. To be heartful is to live from our infinite space, and to enjoy not only an open mind, but an open heart.

References and further reading

1   McKenzie, S and Hassed, C. (2012). *Mindfulness for Life*. Exisle, Wollombi.

CHAPTER 4

What does heartfulness look like, and feel like?

The best and most beautiful things in the world cannot be seen or even touched — they must be felt with the heart.

Helen Keller, The Story of My Life

Does heartfulness only exist in books, or is it real?

If heartfulness is real, how do we recognize
it — in ourselves and in other people?

What does heartfulness look like?

What does heartfulness feel like?

The best way to learn anything is from examples. We know the power of good and bad examples in parenting and in teaching; however, the power of examples isn't just vital to parents and teachers, it is vital to all of us. This chapter offers some powerful positive examples of heartfulness in people who seemed to always have it, and in people who seemed to develop it, and in people who seemed to be powerfully heartful at least once, when it most mattered. These examples are from ancient religions and philosophies, our modern era, and from even closer to our heartful home.

Classical examples of heartfulness

Our great ancient human help systems were all about heartfulness and about the power of positive example, even if that wasn't recognized as such then, or now. These systems give us powerful examples of people living heartfully as well as helping others to live heartfully. These people are not a bunch of human has-beens — they live on, if we let them, in our own heartfulness.

Gautama the Buddha

Gautama the Buddha, or Gotama (Pali spelling) the Buddha, was born in or about 563BC in what was then an independent state in the Himalayan foothills known as the Shakya republic, located in modern Nepal, and he died in about 483BC. Gautama lived the first 29 years of his life as a prince, and then abandoned that life, including his wife and baby son, because he felt that his life and other people's lives lacked true depth, fulfilment and happiness. Gautama went off to the forest on a spiritual quest, which was quite common at that time and place, particularly amongst Brahmins, which Gautama was.

After about six years of seeking, Gautama finally found, or rather he *realized* enlightenment — freedom from suffering — one full-moon night under a

Banyan tree in a village near modern Varanasi. Gautama then spent the rest of his long life being an enlightenment tour guide, showing other people the way to the *dharma*, to the treasure within.

Gautama the Buddha is not *the* Buddha, despite what many of his followers believe, and not a god or anything else that we see as 'out there' rather than 'in here'. Buddha was and is *a* Buddha, because his essential teaching is that we are all Buddhas potentially. We can all *wake up* to our full life potential, by waking up to our life. Gautama the Buddha gave us wonderfully practical ways of achieving happiness and contentment, including the four noble truths and the eight-fold path to enlightenment, and heartfulness. Did he lead by example?

Gautama the Buddha didn't just teach Buddhism, he *experienced* it. A large part of Guatama's 'teaching' was simply his living example of what waking up looks like, and feels like. Gautama the Buddha wasn't an enlightenment expert, he was enlightened. He didn't teach heartfulness, he was heartful. This is a great example of heartfulness, by whatever name. Gautama the Buddha is a true example of how we can find and show heartfulness.

Mary Magdalene

Mary Magdalene is a marvellous mystery. All that we know about her is that she travelled with Jesus as one of his followers, was present at his crucifixion and resurrection, and was mentioned more often in the four Gospels of the New Testament than were most of Jesus' official disciples. There are stories that after the death of Christ Mary Magdalene roamed for many years searching for peace of mind, including by travelling to Egypt. Ancient documents were found in a cave in Egypt that were acquired by a German academic in Cairo in 1896. These documents might be a lost gospel — of Mary Magdalene. This gospel has been interpreted by at least some experts as evidence that Mary was a disciple of Jesus. The possibility has even been mooted that she was Jesus' mistress or wife.

Mary Magdalene's surname translates as 'tower', 'fortress', 'great' and 'magnificent'. She stayed with Jesus at the cross after most of his official disciples had fled, was at his burial, and was the first person to realize that Jesus had risen.

Heartfulness isn't *related* to the Christian message, it *is* the Christian message. Mary Magdalene wasn't an accessory to the Christian message, she lived it. Mary Magdalene is a great living example of how we can find and show heartfulness.

Marcus Aurelius

Marcus Aurelius lived in Rome between 121 and 180AD. He was a philosopher, and no ordinary one, because he was also a Roman Emperor. This unique combination made him a living example of the ideal form of government called for by Socrates and recorded by Plato about 500 years earlier: a philosopher king.

Marcus Aurelius was emperor for the last 19 years of his life, and was considered the last of the 'Five Good Emperors', and was one of the greatest Stoic philosophers. His great philosophical work was written, in Greek, for his own guidance and self-improvement, and was originally called 'to myself'. It is perhaps ironic that a book that has helped many people find peace of mind was written by an emperor while on military campaigns during the last 10 years of his life. Public fans of *Meditations* have included Frederick the Great, John Stuart Mill and Bill Clinton.

Marcus Aurelius's *Meditations* give us some magnificently helpful advice on how to be happy and content on the inside, no matter what is happening on the outside of our lives. Marcus Aurelius's great message, that he was well placed to give us, is about how we can be calm in conflict, by following the natural examples of Nature.

Marcus Aurelius wasn't a philosophy expert, he was a philosopher, and this meant that he loved wisdom — life knowledge — and how it can help us. Marcus Aurelius is a unique and great living example of how we can find and show heartfulness.

Modern examples of heartfulness

Nelson Mandela

Nelson Mandela lived for 95 years between 1918 and 2013; 27 of them in a South African jail, and five of them as South Africa's first black and first fully democratically elected president. Nelson Mandela's life is a wonderful ordinary example of greatness and of great heartfulness. His life wasn't ordinary because it was limited or mundane; it was ordinary because he achieved greatness and great heartfulness without coming from a great heartfulness tradition. His essential life lesson is that no matter what our circumstances, no matter what our adversities, we can achieve greatness

by recognising what is deep in our own heart, and in other people's hearts.

Nelson Mandela wasn't a great human expert, he was a great human. Nelson Mandela is a great and unique living example of how we can find and show heartfulness.

Oprah Winfrey

It might seem strange to describe a modern media superstar as an ordinary example of heartfulness; however, this trans-ordinary person is ordinary in that she didn't inherit her great heartfulness from a religious, philosophical or spiritual heartful tradition, she achieved it.

Oprah Winfrey was born in Mississippi in 1954, and seemingly miraculously transformed extremely poor and difficult origins into the larger-than-life world of a mega media superstar and billionaire. *The Oprah Winfrey Show* (1986–2011) was the highest-rated television programme of its kind ever, and she has been described by the CNN TV network, and others, as the most influential woman in the world. Oprah's TV show accomplishments include a powerful supporting of Barrack Obama, which may have been the difference between his being elected and not being elected president of the United States of America. Is there even more to Oprah Winfrey?

The well-known UK publication *Watkins Mind, Body, Spirit* magazine annually publishes a list of the year's top 100 spiritually influential people, and Oprah Winfrey regularly features in its top 10. This is because, as well as being a political king/queen-maker, Oprah is also a spiritual one, as evidenced by her support of the once-obscure spiritual teacher Eckhart Tolle, which may well have been responsible for his becoming a spiritual superstar. There is also her series of over 30 interviews with Gary Zukov, that great bridge-builder between science and consciousness. Oprah has also helped many other people with important messages to reach a far greater audience than they would otherwise have reached.

Oprah Winfrey is a great *indirect* example of heartfulness, because she has helped the world become more heartful by giving it greater access to great heartfulness examples. She is also a great *direct* example of heartfulness, because her interviewing features a uniquely deep and total connectedness that is not merely heart-to-heart, it is heartfulness-to-heartfulness.

Oprah Winfrey is not a great expert in communication, she is a great communicator. She is a unique and great living example of finding and showing heartfulness.

Some close-to-heartful-home examples

People we know

Think of someone you know who is heartful, or at least more heartful than you are, or more heartful than you think you are! What is their secret? What do they have that you don't, or don't seem to? Do they have anything that you don't have? Do they only have what you have, but have had it for longer? Do they resist it less?

Once we know the value of heartfulness, it is vital for us to find it and grow it, and the best way of finding something in ourselves can be finding it in other people. We all know someone who is heartful, at least occasionally. Maybe it was or is a parent, or other relative, or a dear friend, or a marital or work colleague, or someone else we know well. Maybe it is someone who is able to fully connect or be kind or loving or humorous or wise — no matter what is happening to them.

Maybe you have hardly ever or even never personally met a person who is heartful, at least occasionally. Maybe it is someone that you know *of* rather than know, such as the leader of some organisation or human help system or whatever that you are connected to in some way. Maybe it is the Pope or the Dalai Lama or some other famous wise person who you pay money to see or see for free on television. Maybe it is the person who sells you your bread or beer, and who does it with a deep and connecting smile, and who keeps on smiling at you no matter what is happening to them … Maybe it's anyone … Maybe it's you.

Knowing what heartfulness looks like in other people can help us know what it looks like, and feels like, in ourselves. Having said this, heartfulness is a way out of complexity, not into it, so don't worry about whether you have an example of heartfulness or not, or whether you can describe why it is an example. In the end, heartfulness won't really help us unless we are our own example of it, because other people's solutions are *other* people's solutions, and we all have a unique life opportunity to find our unique path to heartfulness.

Children

If you don't think that you can find or be a great living example of heartfulness, find an example that is so common and so obvious that you can't miss it.

Young children are naturally heartful, because they haven't been exposed to our world's life conditions and conditioning long enough to have lost it. If you ask a young child to instruct you in the art of the heart, they are unlikely to help you out at an intellectual level. If you talk to a child in their own language — of open, free, wondering and wonderful connection at a deeper level than language — they will probably give you a living lesson in what it means to be totally open, connected, joyful, heartful and alive.

A small story

I once took my daughter, Miranda, to a public healing event in a church when she was about two years old. She was an experienced walker but not a jaded one. Walking was a novelty to her, just as everything was a novelty to her. We walked out of the event together, and for some reason that I was much too old to understand she sat down on the grass and started playing with some gumnuts. I was upset by this behaviour, because other people who I walk with are usually far more pragmatic in their walking style. I was upset by what my mind saw as an interruption to our need to do the next thing that we were going to do, which actually wasn't important. I then managed to remember mindfulness and practised it by sitting down on the grass with Miranda and sharing her gumnut adventure. That was handy, because I was writing a book about mindfulness at the time. Attending to the gumnuts rather than my thoughts about our so-called lateness was mindful; however, the motivation to connect with another human with a human need was heartful.

Living examples of the nine paths to heartfulness

Kindness

Gautama the Buddha

Gautama said that he was not a 'stone Buddha'. It is easy to be unaffected by the suffering of others if we don't care about them. It is not quite so easy to be unaffected by the suffering of others when we do care — enough to devote our lives to relieving it. Gautama was essentially kind — kind enough to care about others more than himself.

25

Mary Magdalene

Mary lived the essential Christian message of treating others as we would like others to treat us.

Marcus Aurelius

Marcus Aurelius's teaching and example is that our great power isn't the power to rule over others, or even to rule over ourselves. Our great power is being able to be kind to others and ourselves, no matter what our circumstances.

Nelson Mandela

Nelson Mandela's exceptional kindness was demonstrated by his caring deeply for others throughout his extremely difficult life circumstances, and by his being able to forgive his 'enemies'.

Oprah Winfrey

As well as her more overt accomplishments, Oprah Winfrey is a great philanthropist. Her open-heartedness included making a three-week trip to South Africa in 2004 that resulted in $7 million being donated to seriously underprivileged children and others there, and to her own donation of $40 million and her time to establish the Oprah Winfrey Leadership Academy for Girls.

Someone you know ...

Who do you know who shows heartful kindness in the way they live their life?

Adversity

Gautama the Buddha

One of Gautama's great adversities was that he was born a prince, and didn't have ready access to the wisdom that we can get from being conscious in the grip of suffering. He recognized and overcame this adversity by leaving his princely life, and seeking out heart-opening extreme physical and emotional adversities, which led him to understand, teach and live a 'middle path'.

Mary Magdalene

As well as overcoming and being fuelled by that adversity of Christ's persecution and crucifixion, Mary overcame that adversity by living on without him.

Marcus Aurelius

As with Guatama the Buddha, Marcus Aurelius overcame and was fuelled by the adversity of privilege and power. He also overcame and was fuelled by the

practical problems of being politically powerful, such as forced involvement in military campaigns, schemes and plots.

Nelson Mandela

Nelson Mandela overcame and was fuelled by life circumstances that included 27 years in jail in a small cell. His life circumstances didn't make him bitter or small; they made him generous and large.

Oprah Winfrey

Oprah dramatically overcame and was fuelled by great early life adversities. She was born a black girl in America's 1950s deep south to a single mother. She was brought up by her mother and also by her grandmother, in a poverty so extreme that she sometimes wore dresses made from potato sacks, and was made fun of by other children.

Someone you know ...

Who do you know who has used adversity as a pathway to heartfulness?

Humour

Gautama the Buddha

Gautama displayed the natural good humour and humorousness that comes when you are open, light and heartful. The Buddha used puns and parodies and other light-hearted ways of defusing tensions. An example of the Buddha's humour is:

> *A fool, even though he is associated with a wise man all his life, does not understand the Dhamma [Pali spelling], just as a ladle does not know the taste of soup.* The Dhammapada, *verse 64*

Although this might not come across as riotously hilarious outside its original context, it was certainly intended as a joke. The current Dalai Lama's lightness and wit is a wonderful continuation of Gautama's good humour.

Mary Magdalene

No one has written a book about Mary Magdalene's humour, yet someone has written one about the humour of Christ.[1]

An example of Christ's humour is provided in the New Testament:
> *'The Son of Man came eating and drinking,' Jesus said, 'and they say, "Look, a glutton and a drunkard."'* Mathew: 11:19

Marcus Aurelius

The writings of Marcus Aurelius are full of good humour, and sometimes even good comedy! An example is:

> *... after having fallen into amatory passions, I was cured ...*
> Meditations

Nelson Mandela

> *My dominant memory, however ... is of his humor. The humor was not that of a person who told jokes. Nor was it the 'good old boy' bonhomie of a backslapping politician. Instead, he had a unique ability to respond to any issue with wit and humor — and while you were comfortably laughing, inject some observation or statement that instantly transformed that humor into a searing and sobering challenge.* Blake Bromley[3]

Oprah Winfrey

Oprah consistently demonstrates good humour and lightness of spirit.

Someone you know ...

Who do you know who uses humour as a pathway to heartfulness?

Contentment

Gautama the Buddha

Gautama found a way out of suffering because he found a way to just be rather than struggle to be anything or anybody in particular.

Mary Magdalene

Apparently after many years of wandering and discontent, Mary experienced a deep contentment.

Marcus Aurelius

Marcus Aurelius wrote his *Meditations* to help himself find contentment. He succeeded.

Nelson Mandela

You don't survive and thrive in an extreme environment without a contentment that is even deeper than your environment. As with many of these living example of heartfulness, Nelson Mandela's discontent transformed into contentment.

Oprah Winfrey

Oprah has managed to find contentment even in discontent.

Someone you know ...
Who do you know who has found contentment?

Love

Gautama the Buddha
Love is our greatest motivator and our motivator of greatness. Gautama didn't just preach love as 'loving kindness' or 'compassion to all sentient beings', he practised it, by devoting his life to helping others live it.

Mary Magdalene
Mary lived love as Christ lived love, as greatly evidenced by her being the first to see him when he had risen.

Marcus Aurelius
Like all real philosophers, Marcus Aurelius loved real knowledge — life knowledge — which leads to human happiness and contentment; and he therefore knew real love.

Nelson Mandela
You don't go through what Nelson Mandela went through without the great motivation of great love.

Oprah Winfrey
Oprah's connection with her guests and audience was much more deeply powerful than a media or business relationship, it was fuelled by love.

Someone you know ...
Who do you know who is fired by love?

Courage

Gautama the Buddha
If it isn't courageous to abandon everything you have except a deep calling to find a deep and transferable human happiness truth, what is?

Mary Magdalene
Mary was described in the Gospels as courageous enough to stand by Jesus in his hours of suffering and death, and she was courageous enough to stand by herself beyond that.

Marcus Aurelius
Marcus Aurelius's great courage wasn't expressed by his being able to

successfully face and overcome political and military enemies, it was expressed by his being able to face and overcome his own mind, and its limitations, fears and doubts.

Nelson Mandela

> *I learned that courage was not the absence of fear, but the triumph over it. The brave man is not he who does not feel afraid, but he who conquers that fear.*

Oprah Winfrey

If it doesn't take courage to rise from an extremely underprivileged and difficult childhood to be possibly the most powerful woman in the world, and certainly one of its most spiritually influential ones, what does?

Someone you know …

Who do you know who has lived their life courageously?

Knowledge

Gautama the Buddha

Gautama knew what is really important (who we really are), because he could forget what is unimportant (who we think we are).

Mary Magdalene

Mary had a personal knowledge of Christ and his teaching — that the Kingdom of Heaven is within. When we know who we really are, we can help others be who they really are.

Marcus Aurelius

Marcus Aurelius knew what was and is important, and what was and is unimportant. Like all great philosophers, Marcus Aurelius knew that our greatest knowledge is of ourselves, and of what makes us and other people happy and content — finding what is deeper and more deeply valuable in us than our minds.

Nelson Mandela

Nelson Mandela knew even more than the value of freedom, he knew freedom. Nelson Mandela's jail made him free, because he found a freedom inside himself that no jail could contain.

Oprah Winfrey

Oprah's deep level of connection comes from a deep knowing — how to bring together her early Christian influences and natural humanitarianism. That makes great life, as well as great television.

Someone you know ...

Who do you know who has self-knowledge?

Hope

Gautama the Buddha

If Gautama hadn't been fuelled by a prodigious hope, he would have stayed at home in his palace!

Mary Magdalene

Mary was ready and waiting for Jesus' resurrection because she never lost hope. We can all be resurrected if we don't lose hope.

Marcus Aurelius

If there is hope for a Roman Emperor to become a great lover — of humanity and of truth — there's hope for all of us!

Nelson Mandela

Nelson Mandela hoped for freedom for his people, and then for forgiveness for those who opposed freedom, and his hopes were realized.

Oprah Winfrey

If it doesn't require hope to rise from living as an abused child, constantly beaten for misbehaving, to live as possibly the most powerful woman in the world, and certainly one of its most spiritually influential ones, what does?

Someone you know ...

Who do you know who has found hope as a pathway to heartfulness?

Creativity

All of the people described in these examples created a unique path to heart-fulness.

TAKE-HOME HEARTFULNESS TIPS

Gautama the Buddha

Your purpose in life is to find your purpose and give your whole heart and soul to it.

The way is not in the sky. The way is in the heart.

If you truly loved yourself, you could never hurt another.

Mary Magdalene

What is hidden from you I will proclaim to you.

For where the mind is, there is the treasure.

I have recognized that the All is being dissolved, both the earthly things and the heavenly.

She turned their hearts to the Good.

Marcus Aurelius

Confine yourself to the present.

Look within. Within is the fountain of good, and it will ever bubble up, if thou wilt ever dig.

Accept the things to which fate binds you, and love the people with whom fate brings you together, but do so with all your heart.

Nelson Mandela

To be free is not merely to cast off one's chains, but to live in a way that respects and enhances the freedom of others.

A good head and a good heart are always a formidable combination.

I am not a saint, unless you think of a saint as a sinner who keeps on trying.

Oprah Winfrey

Passion is energy. Feel the power that comes from focusing on what excites you.

What you focus on expands, and when you focus on the goodness in your life, you create more of it.

If the heart has not healed, it means it is not ready to move on.

Someone you know ...

The bottomless line

Before you respond to an important life event, or even an unimportant life event that you think is important, ask yourself how a heartful person would respond, then respond as they would. The heartful person might be someone

who you know of, or know, or it might even be you.

The next section of *Heartfulness* further explores the nine paths introduced in Chapter 2.

References and further reading

1   Trueblood, E. (1964). *The Humor of Christ.* Harper and Row, New York.

2   King, K. (2003). *The Gospel of Mary of Magdala: Jesus and the First Woman Apostle.* Polebridge Press, Santa Roas, CA.

3   Bromley, B. 'The humor of Nelson Mandela', posted on the internet, 12 September 2013.

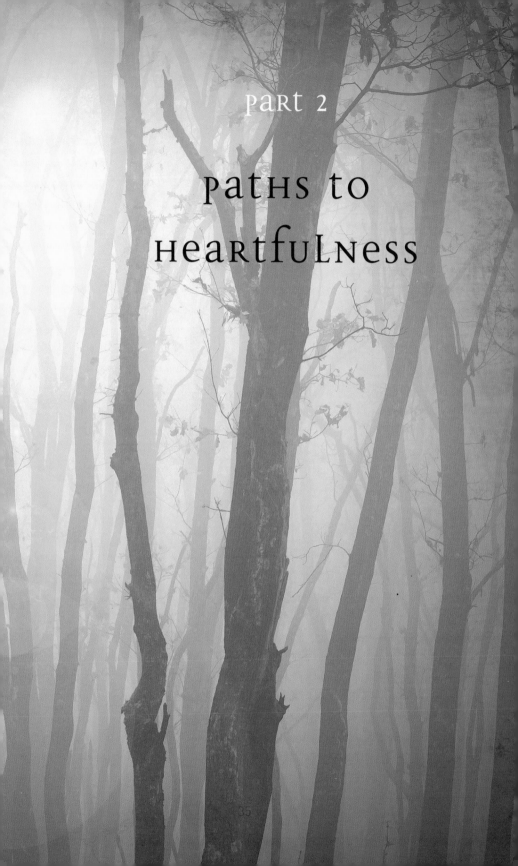

part 2

paths to
heartfulness

CHAPTER 5

Kindness

Be kind whenever possible. It is always possible.

Dalai Lama

What is kindness?

What is it like?

Is kindness fashionable?

Is kindness important?

Is kindness essential?

Kindness might seem like a very small thing in what might seem like a very big world full of very big problems. However, our very big world is made up of things that are so small we can't see them, such as subatomic particles, as well as the infinitely large spaces that allow small things to grow into big things. Something as small as kindness can grow into something as big as love — when we recognize it and allow it.

What is kindness?

Be a rainbow in someone else's cloud.
Maya Angelou, Letter to My Daughter

The online Oxford dictionary defines kindness as:

a behaviour marked by ethical characteristics, a pleasant disposition, and concern for others. It is known as a virtue, and recognized as a value in many cultures and religions.

The philosopher Friedrich Nietzsche described kindness and love as the 'most curative herbs and agents in human intercourse'.

If you still don't quite feel confident that you understand kindness, as well as know it, you could consider the description given by the great Taoist philosopher Lao Tzu about 2500 years ago:

Kindness in words creates confidence.
Kindness in thinking creates profoundness.
Kindness in giving creates love.

Understanding what kindness *is not* might also help us understand what it is. So what are some opposites of kindness? How about:

- unkindness
- selfishness
- ambition
- anger
- blame
- egotism, and
- hard-heartedness.

What are some allies of kindness? How about:

- gentleness
- patience
- forgiveness
- gratitude
- generosity
- empathy, and
- open-heartedness.

Kindness is closely related to love, and can be a lot safer. Kindness can also be a great way of realising our deep connection with other people, especially if love seems too challenging. Love actually isn't challenging, it's the opposite of challenging; however, our *idea* of it can be. The well-known spiritual teacher and power-of-now advocate Eckhart Tolle rarely uses the word 'love' because he thinks it can be explosive. Buddhist philosophy and theology have similar concerns, and usually talk about 'loving kindness' rather than 'love'.

Loving someone who has just cut us off in traffic, or terminated a romantic or employment relationship with us, or dropped something on our foot, can be challenging. Being kind to someone who has just done something we don't like might not be quite as challenging, even if that someone was *us*. The more we practise kindness, even to people who don't deserve it — *especially to people who don't deserve it* — the more we realize that being kind to other

people is being kind to ourselves. Practising kindness is a bit like practising love with training wheels on, because doing something easy can later help us do something hard. Kindness, however, is much more than a poor relative of love, because when we naturally and consistently feel our natural flow of kindness, no matter how small it seems, we connect with a truly great and greatly accessible power.

Kindness and heartfulness

> *I feel no need for any other faith than my faith in the kindness of human beings. I am so absorbed in the wonder of earth and the life upon it that I cannot think of heaven and angels.* Pearl S Buck

Kindness causes heartfulness and is caused by heartfulness. When we are kind we connect with our deep inner space, and we connect with other people's deep inner space, at our shared heart. When we find the source of our deep human connection we are no longer lost in space, because we have found our way home. To better know kindness, we can look at kindnesses from ourselves and from others.

> **What was the first kind thing that you did today?**
> **What was the first kind thing that someone**
> **you know did today?**

These questions are not meant to inspire you to accuse people of not being kind; they are meant to inspire you to recognize that kindness, like oxygen, is vital to us and it is everywhere, even if we don't see it.

The first kind thing that I did today was to close the bedroom door of my four-year-old daughter, Miranda, so that my early-morning work on this chapter wouldn't wake her, even though I don't usually write particularly noisily.

Another recent act of — or rather *expression of* — kindness that I can remember was so microscopic that I might not even have noticed it without a microscopic mindfulness or heartfulness detector. Yesterday my wife Melanie's church fête quartet ('Holy Strung') was given $50 towards church building

works by a grateful listener. When Melanie told me about this financial wind-fall, an unkind voice in my mindless mind or heartless heart was just about to say something glib or dismissive such as: 'You'll only have to play for another 17 years to pay for the new stained-glass window' or even 'They should have given you $100 to stop playing!' Fortunately these dangerous thoughts were noticed before they were unleashed, and were replaced with 'Sometimes $50 is worth a lot more than $50.'

A recent act of kindness to myself happened last night when I was having trouble making a decision about whether to work on a kindness chapter, or write a radio script, or write a mindfulness/heartfulness talk, or do some work for my official job. Rather than conducting a raffle to find a work winner, I turned off my computer and went to bed.

Can you think of something that you or someone else did or said recently that was kinder than what could have been done or said? Kindness seeds are like oak tree seeds: they can grow into something great if we water them with our attention.

What are the vital ingredients of kindness?

Consider your own example of kindness or the examples given above. What makes them examples of kindness? How about:

- **being aware that someone needs us to be kind**
- **accepting the value of the person who needs kindness**
- **being aware of the consequences of our kindness or our lack of kindness**
- **knowing or at least imagining what the other person is experiencing**
- **accepting our response-ability for the effects we have on other minds and hearts, and through them on *our* mind and heart?**

These core ingredients of kindness are vital ingredients for our *connection* with other people and with ourselves. We have our best and only opportunity to practise kindness right here and right now, with whoever is with us right here and right now. Our best and only opportunity to learn what kindness is, and how it can cause and be caused by heartfulness, is to practise it, and to keep practising it. Our best and only way of knowing kindness and its power is to feel it. We can practise kindness even when we think there are plenty of good reasons not to, and the harder it is to do something the more powerful it is when we do it. Like all good behaviours that seem bad or pointless or even impossible at first, the more we do them the easier they get, and the better they get.

The benefits of kindness

What wisdom can you find that is greater than kindness?
Jean-Jacques Rousseau, Émile

There is plenty of scientific evidence that supports our common-sense belief that opposites of kindness — such as anger and blame — harm their perpetuators, as well as their apparent targets. There is also scientific evidence that kindness gives the people who transmit it, as well as the people who receive it, many important benefits.

Piero Ferrucci is a transpersonal psychologist who wrote a book called *The Power of Kindness: The Unexpected Benefits of Leading a Compassionate Life.*[1] Ferrucci's book provides strong evidence that kindness is a trait that leads to happiness and eventually love, in us, in the people around us, and in a world that has become 'cold, anxious, difficult, and frightening'. Ferrucci makes the important point that being kind doesn't mean being a 'human doormat' or being 'falsely kind', such as out of fear or a desire to get something we want. Kindness is actually made up of many elements, including flexibility, honesty, trust, patience, loyalty, a sense of belonging, gratitude, attention and forgiveness. According to Piero Ferrucci, kindness is not a luxury, it is a necessity.

The results of a systematic review of 22 scientific studies on the benefits of

kindness or loving kindness meditation were recently reported in the *Journal of Consulting and Clinical Psychology*.[2] This study by Julieta Galante and her colleagues showed that a formal practice of kindness decreased people's depression levels, and increased their compassion, mindfulness, wellbeing, health and social interaction levels. Research by Inga Boellinghaus and others[3] showed that loving kindness meditation increases 'self-compassion' and 'focused concern' in therapists and other health professionals. This has important benefits, including the strengthening of relationships with clients, and reducing stress and burn-out. Although these techniques are typically described as 'mindfulness', a better description may well be 'heartfulness' because at their heart is our deep human connection.

Kindness in action

- The next time you think that what someone just did to you or in spite of you is unforgivable, forgive them. Forgive someone who you think least deserves it and who you realize most needs it. This someone may have just cut you off in traffic or ended a relationship ... This someone could even be you.

- The next time you are about to blame someone for something they did or did not do, feel some space, feel some grace, feel some heart and feel some heartfulness. Don't let yourself be contracted by your ideas about what should be — nothing should be anything other than what it is. Let the grace space expand and keep expanding ...

- Be gentle with yourself and with other people. Don't criticize yourself or other people even in your mind. Criticising means judging and separating. What starts off so small that you can hardly see it can grow to infect your entire world. We often criticize people because we want them to change, but that's not how they see our criticism: they see it as hostility. We change others when we change ourselves. We are kind to others when we are kind to ourselves.

TAKE-HOME TIPS

- Be kind to people even when you think they don't deserve it, *especially* when you think they don't deserve it.

- Be kind to yourself even when you think you don't deserve it, *especially* when you think you don't deserve it.

- Recognize that the source of your unkindness is your own thoughts about what happened, not what happened.

- Realize that it can be as hard being the person who you are angry with, or fearful of, or upset about, as it can be being you.

- Don't wait to be kind to someone else until someone else is kind to you.

Examples of the kind path to heartfulness

There are plenty of big examples of kindness and the heartfulness-expanding benefits it gives the giver as well as the receiver, and there are plenty of small examples, too.

the Last kindness Leaf

A literary and cinematic great act of kind heartfulness that reveals something great and deep in all of us was *The Last Leaf*. This was a movie based on a story published in 1907 by a once-famous American short-story writer called O. Henry. In *The Last Leaf* a young woman was dying of pneumonia, or thought she was, and she decided that when the wind blew the last leaf off the tree she was watching she would die. That night there was a storm, and it was obvious that no leaves could have survived it; however, when the curtain was pulled back it revealed that a leaf had indeed survived, and so did the young woman. Yet an old artist friend of hers died of pneumonia, after painting his finest picture — that of a last leaf.

Recently, I experienced something similar when a beautiful frangipani flower blew onto the windscreen my family's rent-a-car in Cairns. It survived long enough to inspire us.

KINDNESS at HOME

A recent kindness example that is so small that you might not see it without a heartful microscope is that of my young daughter who hates capsicums. Instead of telling this to a person who had kindly cooked her a meal full of capsicums, she said that she was full. This tiny kindness example has quantum power because our kindness universe is made up of its micro particles.

KINDNESS away from HOME

'Small' examples of kindness include the many things we do every day for the people we love. Perhaps even greater examples of the kind path to heartfulness, or the heartful path to kindness, are the kind things that we do for people whom we don't love, don't know, or even don't like. I was once stuck in a four-wheel-drive vehicle on a crowded and rickety bridge late one night in India, with two young women and two young children.

It was noisy and hot, and it seemed as though we were surrounded by strangers and strangeness, which soon all became hostile and threatening in my increasingly rampant imagination. Then something in me opened — an awareness, a new way of seeing, a heartfulness. I suddenly realized that we spend most of our time among strangers, and that we are protected by the strange fact that most of us are mostly kind to each other most of the time. I suddenly felt trust: we were on this broken bridge together, and I felt a certainty that we would all be alright … We were.

The kindness bottomless line

Where is the last place that you would look for your own or someone else's kindness, if you think it is missing? What if kind heartfulness lives in the last place we would think to look for it — in what looks like its opposite? If we follow anything to its source, we will find what we are looking for. We can transcend the opposite of kindness rather than defend it, by finding or creating an oasis of kindness in disconnection deserts.

References and further reading

1   Ferrucci, P. (2006). *The Power of Kindness: The Unexpected Benefits of Leading a Compassionate Life.* Penguin, New York.

2   Galante, J, Bekkers, M and Gallacher, M. (2014). Effect of kindness-based meditation on health and well-being: A systematic review and meta-analysis. *Journal of Consulting and Clinical Psychology*, 82(6): 1101–1114.

3   Boellinghaus, I, Jones, F and Hutton, J. (2014). The role of mindfulness and loving-kindness meditation in cultivating self-compassion and other-focused concern in health care professionals. *Mindfulness*, 5(2): 129–138.

CHAPTER 6

Adversity

Sweet are the uses of adversity.

William Shakespeare, As You Like It, *Act 2, Scene 1*

Great challenges require great responses.

What if the bottom has just fallen out of your
world, or it seems like it has?

What if it seems like you have just lost something
vital and irreplaceable, such as your job, or a relationship,
or your health?

What if you have lost heart?

Is this the end, or the beginning?

The German philosopher Friedrich Nietzsche famously said 'What doesn't kill me makes me stronger.' This principle is also the active ingredient of immunizations against diseases such as chicken pox and tuberculosis, and of homeopathy and the hair-of-the-dog hangover cure. These procedures all give us a very small dose of something that would hurt us in its full dose, in order to make us strong enough to become immune to the full version. Does this also work for our life adversities? Can things that we would never have chosen, such as extremely challenging life circumstances, actually benefit us by giving us more depth, empathy and resilience? Can our adversities force us to find a way home, to our lost heart and heartfulness?

Many things don't have obvious meanings or easy answers. Does adversity, and the suffering that it can lead to, have a non-obvious positive purpose? Does adversity have to lead to suffering? If it doesn't, is there something useful we can learn from the difference between when it does and when it doesn't? Can adversity benefit us in some marvellously mysterious way?

A well-known cardinal (George Pell) and an even more well-known aetheist (Richard Dawkins) once debated each other on television, in what proved to be more of an intellectual brawl than a debate. During it, someone in the audience asked Cardinal Pell a challenging question: 'If there is a God, and if God created everything, why did he create suffering?' Cardinal Pell conceded that this is a notoriously tricky point, and Richard Dawkins graciously allowed him to deal with it alone. Cardinal Pell answered by saying that suffering can be good for us: in a deep and mysterious way, it can help us grow into what we really are.

If this is true, then maybe some forms of suffering at least might be useful in

some way to at least some of us, sometimes, and maybe suffering can even help us connect with other people and with our true life purpose and potential. Are Shakespeare's sweet uses of adversity the opening of our minds and of our hearts?

What is adversity?

Every cloud has a silver lining. Proverb

When we really see the clouds, we really see the light beyond them.

The Oxford online dictionary defines 'adversity' as 'a difficult or unpleasant situation'. Does this sound like something that *doesn't have to* lead to a blind or heartless reaction? Is adversity the same for all of us, or does its meaning depend on the state of our minds and hearts, and on their connectedness?

Is it an adversity when we don't get the beautiful new toy we wanted as a child, or the beautiful new boy- or girlfriend we wanted as a teenager, or the beautiful new job we wanted as an adult? What if we have a health or financial or relationship problem and we are feeling discomfort or pain (emotional or physical) — is this adversity? Maybe if we see adversity as misfortune, calamity or distress, it leads to suffering — but do we have to see it that way?

What then is suffering? If you *don't* know what suffering is, congratulations (or commiserations!) Here is a dictionary definition to help give you an idea of what you have missed out on: 'the act of someone who suffers'.[1]

Maybe an important reason why at least one dictionary doesn't even seriously try to define suffering is that it doesn't really mean anything to anyone who hasn't experienced it. If you don't think you know what suffering is, then think of a time when you wanted to be doing something other than what you were doing. The comedian Stan Laurel was asked by one of his nurses when he was dying how he was: 'I'd rather be skiing,' he replied. 'So you're a skier, then, Mr Laurel?' 'No!'

Try multiplying the feeling you experienced when you thought you would rather be doing something else until you can understand the suffering of people who leave their job, or relationship, or even life to avoid it. Do we suffer

because our life situation forces us to suffer, or because we *react* to our life situation by closing our minds and our hearts and our heartfulness?

Is there an adversity alchemy?

Can we transform our extreme life events from causes of suffering to causes of heartfulness?

If we can, how can we?

Heartfulness and adversity

What makes the desert beautiful is that somewhere it hides a well.
Antoine de Saint-Exupéry, The Little Prince

Overcoming adversity is the theme of many great works of literature, theatre, cinema, music, comedy and life. Victor Hugo's *Les Misérables* is a great example of all of these genres. Its hero — Jean Valjean (John Johnson in English) — was damaged physically, psychologically and spiritually by some dramatically challenging life circumstances. These circumstances closed his mind and his heart until he was consumed by his suffering, and felt like a sufferer rather than a human who was suffering.

Jean Valjean stole a loaf of bread to feed his hungry family in pre-French Revolution France, and ended up doing many years of hard time as a galley slave for his 'crime'. When he was eventually released, he was so broken, bitter and damaged that he barely recognized the grace of his deeper undamaged humanity. This was revealed to him by the acts of kindness of a priest who gave him food and eventually valuable silver candlesticks to save him from being arrested again. The point of this story, and others like it, is that somehow Jean Valjean finally recognized the grace of his deep, undamaged humanity, which showed that at heart he hadn't actually been destroyed. His adversity kept deepening until he was either strengthened or destroyed, there was no other choice.

Saint Paul pointed out that sometimes it is our weakness that makes us strong. The yoga of desperation is also about how our life can seem so overwhelmingly

bad that we can't go on, and then something transforms in us and we are deeply happy, apparently for no reason. The reason is that we can find our deep life answers in our heart when we have nowhere else to go. The great Buddhist writer Pema Chödrön pointed out in her *The Places That Scare You*[2] that when we finally realize that what we can't escape in our hearts and the hearts that they are connected to, we blossom into what we truly are. William Shakespeare and Eckhart Tolle also pointed out that things aren't as bad as we think:

> *There is nothing either good or bad, but thinking makes it so.*
> William Shakespeare, Hamlet, Act 2, Scene 2

> *The cause of your unhappiness is never what you think it is.*
> Eckhart Tolle

We think that we suffer because we don't have what we want, or we have what we don't want. Is this true? Is it avoidable? Suffering is a word, not a sentence — it is a mind-made condition, not a divine decree. We are the gatekeepers of our hearts and minds: we can choose how to respond to what is happening around us. For example, our minds habitually add their own spin to our experiences, such as 'This is a catastrophe!' But it isn't necessarily so: it's just what we think it is. Our thoughts are caused by and cause our emotions. Our minds are connected to our hearts, and when we lose heart, we can lose our mind. We don't have to lose anything, when we realize that we never lose what's most important — our essence.

The benefits of adversity

> *Adversity is the first path to truth.*
> Lord Byron, Don Juan

There is strong scientific evidence that our life events can damage our mind, our body and our connectedness. There is also strong scientific evidence that our life events *don't have to damage us*, and they can even help us experience life more deeply, valuably and heartfully.

Stress — particularly long-term stress — can hurt just about every bit of us that can hurt or otherwise malfunction. Suffering often results in long-term stress, which leads to our immune system malfunctioning, our arteries hardening, high blood pressure, bone-thinning, loss of brain cells and premature ageing. Suffering can also cause serious psychological problems, such as anxiety and depression, which are increasingly common destinations in our society.

There is also a budding body of scientific evidence that shows that extreme life events — our adversities — can actually help us, psychologically, physically, spiritually and heartfully. Whether our life events close us down or open us up depends on how we respond to them.

Optimism is a psychological capacity or a spiritual practice or a gift from the gods that is closely related to hope. The great positive psychology proponent Professor Martin Seligman published his highly successful *Learned Optimism*[4] as a follow-up to his equally successful *Learned Helplessness*.[5] Scientific studies have shown that our ability to thrive in adversity is related to our level of optimism.[6]

Resilience is a psychological capacity or a spiritual practice or a gift from the gods that is related to optimism and hope, and is also a key to positive psychology. Resilient people can face all kinds of extreme difficulties and remain optimistic, happy and healthy. Non-resilient people can face all kinds of extreme non-difficulties and instantly lose hope, happiness and health. What is the difference? Scientific studies have shown that life difficulties can help us develop resilience, rather than result in psychological and physical damage such as post-traumatic stress disorders.[7,8] This phenomenon is a psychological and a heartful equivalent to the medical model of immunisation, which builds physical resilience by giving people a version of a disease that is small enough for them to overcome. Similarly, learning to deal effectively with psychological small stuff helps us to deal effectively with the large stuff.

Moreover, scientific studies have shown that at least sometimes the difference between what strengthens us and what damages us is how much support we get from other people, especially when we are young.[9] Children with mental and physical problems whose parents, community or other key life players show a positive attitude are much more likely to thrive than children whose key life players show a negative attitude. This thriving isn't just mental and

physical, it goes deeper, and includes an ability to live deeply and valuably — heartfully. Scientific studies have also shown that mindfulness/heartfulness can protect adults from being damaged by their childhood adversities, which approximately two-thirds of children experience, and also make them healthier than adults who did not experience them.[10]

The scientific studies described above even support our common sense: adversity can, at least sometimes, deepen our humanity. We can add heart to Nietzsche's famous quote: *What I don't close my heart to helps me grow.*

Adversity in action

- Allow adversity to strengthen and deepen you. The best places and spaces for us to learn and to grow aren't necessarily comfortable and calm and safe, because these places don't necessarily challenge us to find resources deep within ourselves.

- Allow adversity to help you find out something new about yourself. A great thing about any newness in our lives, even if we think it is a disaster, is that it can help us come alive: it can *stimulate* us or even shock us out of our life lethargy. This might be why there is such a fine line between an adventure and an ordeal. Sometimes we need to leave our idea of home to find our real home. Sometimes adversity reminds us that we are alive.

- Realize that we don't live or suffer alone. No matter what our adversity is or seems to be, we are facing it with others because we are essentially linked with others. This link is the cause and the cure of our suffering.

No man is an island,
Entire of itself …
Any man's death diminishes me,
Because I am involved in mankind.
And therefore never send to know
For whom the bell tolls;
It tolls for thee.
John Donne, No Man is an Island

TAKE-HOME TIPS

- Allow adversity to open your life and your heart, not close it.

- Let the suffering buck stop with you. Don't think that reacting to challenging events by making other people suffer more will make you suffer less.

- Welcome adversities as challenges, rather than resist them as disasters.

Examples of the adverse path to heartfulness

Eckhart Tolle wrote in *A New Earth* that suffering can help us achieve, or prevent us from achieving, our full human potential, depending on whether we suffer consciously or unconsciously.[11] We have a choice about whether or not we listen to our life calling. Unconscious suffering leads to more suffering, such as when someone treads on our toe (literally or metaphorically) and we blindly react by treading on two of their toes. In this way the whole world can end up in a suffering chain-reaction. How, then, do we stop passing the suffering buck? There are plenty of real-life and not quite-so-real-life examples of people suffering unconsciously, and also some examples of people suffering consciously. You might even be able to think of some examples in your own life. The following is a good real-life example of how adversity can lead us to heartfulness.

a ceo's Recovery

A newly elected CEO of a well-known state rather liked his job. Being a state CEO can be extremely satisfying, and this particular CEO thoroughly enjoyed it. As with most people in public positions, however, being watched by millions of other people as you are doing what you are doing can have its challenges.

Eventually the state CEO lost an apparently un-losable election, and developed depression in response to this perceived adversity. The now ex-head of state responded heartfully to his apparent adversity by seeking to understand what caused it. This powerful reflective process eventually led to his opening his heart and helping numerous other people open their hearts when he became the head of a highly valuable national organisation focused on improving mental health. This organisation helps people with mental illness by giving them information about their illness, raising public awareness of mental illness, and researching new treatments for it.

Two more examples of the potential benefits of adversity are provided by two special American presidents.

fDR's flowering

Franklin Roosevelt developed infantile paralysis (polio) when he was 39. This condition could have spelt the end of his promising political career, or to its blossoming. In 1933, 12 years after developing polio and being confined to a wheelchair, Franklin Roosevelt was elected President of the United States of America, and went on to serve an unprecedented three terms. Not only that, he led the United States successfully through two of its greatest ever challenges: the Great Depression and the Second World War. People who knew Franklin Roosevelt before and after he contracted polio believed that he didn't become a great president despite the adversity of his physical disability, but because of it.[12] In their words:

He was disciplined by his illness. Robert Jackson, Supreme Court Justice

Roosevelt underwent a spiritual transformation during the years of his illness. I noticed when he came back that the years of pain and suffering had purged the slightly arrogant attitude he had displayed on occasion before he was stricken. The man emerged completely warm hearted, with a humility of spirit and with a deeper philosophy ... I saw Roosevelt only once between 1921 and 1924, and I was instantly struck by his growth. He was young, he was crippled, he was physically weak, but he had a firmer grip on life and on himself than ever before. Frances Perkins, friend of FDR

jfk's challenges

John Fitzgerald Kennedy was faced, like Gautama the Buddha, with the potentially especially insidious human adversity of being born into a rich and powerful family. Also like Gautama the Buddha, JFK transcended that adversity, in his own way, by becoming even more rich and powerful. His elevation in life status actually deepened and evolved his humanity, rather than gave him an inflated idea of himself that he could never satisfy. JFK was also faced with great physical and psychological health adversities that could easily have destroyed his body and mind, rather than inspire him to transcend them.

Although it was suppressed at the time, JFK suffered from a condition that was often fatal before the discovery of cortisone: Addison's disease. This disease affected JFK's immune system so that he didn't have adequate levels of the naturally occurring steroids that allow us to ward off infections. He almost died of complications arising from this condition several times, including early in his presidency, before he was finally diagnosed and properly treated. JFK also had severe back pain caused by chronic muscle spasms, and he experienced episodes of depression as a young man. None of these conditions destroyed JFK; rather, they made him stronger, until he was not only the youngest elected president of the United States (at age 43), but, after a shaky start caused by incorrect use of the steroids used to treat him, he went on to become a great president.

Early in his presidency, JFK was monstered by the Soviet Premier Nikita Krushchev, was described as weak, and made a mess of the Cuban Bay of Pigs military misadventure. He had great attributes, however — great resilience and a great ability to learn life lessons. In 1963, he helped save the world from nuclear war when he showed that he had learned from the Bay of Pigs episode to not allow military people to make military decisions. Instead, he handled the Cuban missile crisis himself — creatively, calmly and correctly — when missiles aimed at America were installed only 150 kilometres from Miami.

JFK also saved the world from post-war ennui when he came to be perceived as a modern King Arthur, whose Washington court was seen as a modern Camelot. If he hadn't been assassinated in his prime in late 1963 by powerful organisational enemies, who set up Lee Harvey Oswald as a scarcely convincing fall-guy, the world may well have not had to endure the Vietnam War. Perhaps JFK didn't become great in spite of his adversities, but because of them.

There are many famous examples of people responding heartfully to their adversity and inspiring others to respond heartfully to theirs. There are also many close-to-home examples. Have you ever responded to something seemingly going hideously wrong, such as losing your relationship or job or good health, by looking deeply into yourself and finding something worth finding?

True examples of the courage and heroism of heartful responses to large and small adversities are everywhere, and in every time. Maybe you are a parent and you are spending a lot of your time doing things that you wouldn't necessarily be doing if you weren't doing it for somebody other than yourself. Maybe you are working in a job that inspires you to do it for more than just you. Maybe you are working on yourself and you are starting with trying to be just a little bit better in some way than you were yesterday … A great journey can begin with a single thought.

The adversity bottomless line

How can we transform our adversities from blatant disasters into disguised blessings? As with fame, some of us seem to have suffering thrust upon us, while

others of us seem to achieve it! Some people even seem to enjoy suffering, or at least identify so strongly with it that if you suggest to them that they don't need it they will get angry and offended. Maybe the first step towards transforming our adversities from causes of damage to opportunities for happiness and freedom is recognising that at some point in our response to it we have a choice.

The bottomless line of our adversity–heartfulness balance sheet, then, is whether or not we can profit from our adversity. Is there a cosmic compensation available to us if we can wake up to our deep life opportunities? Can we be life puppeteers as well as puppets? Are our adversities at least sometimes telling us something we need to know, and can these messages be our greatest life-opening opportunities? The answers are in our heart and in our common human heart — our heartfulness.

References and further reading

1   *Macquarie Concise Dictionary* (4th edn) (2006). Macquarie Dictionary Publishers, Sydney.

2   Chödrön, P. (2001). *The Places That Scare You: A Guide to Fearlessness*. Shambhala, Boston.

3   McKenzie, S and Hassed, C. (2012). *Mindfulness for Life*. Exisle, Wollombi.

4   Seligman, M. (1991). *Learned Optimism: How to Change Your Mind and Your Life*. Knopf, New York.

5   Seligman, M. (1975). *Helplessness: On Depression, Development, and Death*. WH Freeman, San Francisco.

6   Buchanan, G and Seligman, M (eds). (1995). *Explanatory Style*. Lawrence Erlbaum Associates, Hillsdale, NJ.

7   Masten, AS. (2011). Resilience in children threatened by extreme adversity: Frameworks for research, practice, and translational synergy. *Development and Psychopathology*, 23(2): 493–506.

8   Seery, MD, Leo, RJ, Lupien, SP, Kondrak, CL and Almonte, JL. (2013). An upside to adversity? Moderate cumulative lifetime adversity is associated with resilient responses in the face of controlled stressors. *Psychological Science*, 24(7): 1181.

9   Bugental, DB. (2004). Thriving in the face of early adversity. *Journal of Social Issues*, 60(1): 219–235.

10 Whitaker, R, Dearth-Wesley, T, Gooze, RA, Becker, BD, Gallagher, KC and McEwen, BS. (2014). Adverse childhood experiences, dispositional mindfulness, and adult health. *Preventive Medicine*, 67: 147–153.

11 Tolle, E. (2005). *A New Earth: Awakening to Your Life's Purpose*. Penguin, New York.

12 Ghaemi, N. (2011). *A First-rate Madness: Uncovering the Links Between Leadership and Mental Illness*. Penguin, London, at pp. 142–143.

CHAPTER 7

Humour

There's no life without humour. It can make the
wonderful moments of life truly glorious, and it can
make tragic moments bearable. *Rufus Wainwright*

When humor works, it works because it's clarifying
what people already feel. It has to come from
someplace real. *Tina Fey*

Experience has shown, and a true philosophy will
always show, that a vast, perhaps the larger portion
of the truth arises from the seemingly irrelevant.

Edgar Allan Poe, The Mystery of Marie Rogêt

What is humour?

What is humour for?

Is there something deep and deeply necessary about
humour as well as something laughably light?

Can humour help reconnect us with what is vital to us, that
we might not have even noticed our lost connection with?

Is humour the ultimate cop-out or the ultimate cop-in?

Is humour real?

Humour has been around for a long time, maybe for as long as there have been people to appreciate it, or even longer. Does humour exist because we like it, or does it exist because we need it, or both? We might not think of humour as a deep and deeply necessary human attribute, we might think of it as a joke; however, there are great examples of humour helping people live and enjoy living when things seemed unendurable, or at least unenjoyable. As with science and philosophy, humour often starts with a question:

What came first, the chicken or the egg?

How did human life originate?

Who am I?

As it happens, all three of these great inquiries can be answered by an answer to the first question: neither, because what came first was life, before it was formed into anything.

Let's begin our exploration of how humour can take us to heartfulness, and how heartfulness can take us to humour, by looking at the questions that opened this chapter. The punchline is that we might not find definite answers to these questions on our way to answering our main question, or we might. Our main question is:

Can humour be our greatest hidden heartful resource?

When I was about eleven, my teacher told my class that having a sense of

humour is the most valuable thing that we can have. I didn't believe him — maybe I was already conditioned to believe that the really valuable things in life, such as hard work, stress and doubt, are *serious*, and things such as play and fun and humour are not valuable rather than invaluable. I presented my teacher's humour hypothesis to my mother after school, and much to my surprize she told me that Mr Morgan was right: humour is our most valuable gift. I have been pondering that idea ever since, and I have managed to come up with some very *serious* ideas about how humour can help us live our lives happily and heartfully, and also some very *light* ones.

What is humour?

> *Humour is the weapon of unarmed people: it helps people who are*
> *oppressed to smile at the situation that pains them.*
> Simon Wiesenthal

Maybe humour just *is*, like life, laugher and love, but what is it? The Oxford online dictionary defines it as 'the quality of being amusing or comic, especially as expressed in literature or speech'.

Does that help? A problem with words is that they are only symbols of what is real rather than being real in themselves — they are tools for expressing something rather than the something they are trying to express. This is particularly true of humour.

The word 'humour' is derived from ancient Greek medicine's adoption of what was probably a much older Egyptian idea: that we are made up of four humours. Some ancient Greek medicos, such as Hippocrates, linked these four humours to the four elements — earth, fire water and air. Being classified as having a particular humour means being classified as having a high concentration of the qualities associated with it, and a corresponding need to keep them in balance. This division of our humours into four types underpinned the origin of psychological theories of personality (from the Roman word *personae* — mask) as well as the origin of the word humour.

Humour

Type	Element	Description
Sanguine	Air	Courageous, hopeful, playful, carefree
Choleric	Fire	Ambitious, leader-like, restless, easily angered
Melancholic	Earth	Despondent, quiet, analytical, serious
Phlegmatic	Water	Calm, thoughtful, patient, peaceful

Over time, the word 'humour' has come to mean good humour, and maybe we can all be good-humoured (as in sanguine or even phlegmatic) if we can let go of some of our ambition, restlessness, anger, despondence, over-analysis and seriousness!

Humour, or at least a particular type of humour, is related to the word 'wit', which originated in the Old English word *wit*, or *witt*, which meant understanding or mental capacity, or consciousness; and is related to the word 'wisdom'. The modern meaning of 'wit', as in 'ability to connect ideas and express them in an amusing way', was apparently first recorded in the 1540s.[1]

Wit and humour can both involve our seeing things in a different way. Have you ever seen something in your life as going badly and then worse, and then you actually felt better when things seemed worse because they seemed so bad that they were funny? Maybe you suddenly felt light because your reaction to something happening in your life was so heavy that you had to drop it. Maybe when you saw the lightness you saw the light, because you saw the darkness differently. Maybe humour, like love, frees us from what we think.

Theories of humour

I have never understood why it should be considered derogatory to the Creator to suppose that he has a sense of humour.
Dean William Ralph Inge, 'Confessio Fideo', Outspoken Essays

People have come up with wonderfully complicated and contradictory theories about just about everything. These theories include theories of the human

mind and the human body and their interrelationship — a sacred and deeply harmonious marriage, or a shotgun wedding? Why, then, shouldn't we also have theories about something as important to our happiness, health and heartfulness as humour?

Arthur Koestler was a great Hungarian–British writer who was made a Commander of the Order of the British Empire (CBE), and who also found time to give us a wonderfully complicated theory of humour, and how it relates to creativity.[2] According to Koestler, at least, humour manifests as laughter when:

> ... *the collision of two matrices and, particularly, when the self-assertive aggressive-defensive emotions are involved. These emotions tend to beget bodily activity since 'due to their greater inertia and persistence' cannot keep up with the swift bisociative act.*
>
> *Laughter is a luxury reflex which could arise only in a creature whose reason has gained a degree of autonomy from the urges of emotion, and enables him to perceive his own emotions as redundant — to realize that he has been fooled.*
>
> The Act of Creation, *p. 96*

Don't worry if all that's not fully clear yet, because Koestler gives us a wonderfully complicated joke to illustrate his theory:

> *Chamfort tells a story of a Marquis at the court of Lousis XIV who, on entering his wife's boudoir and finding her in the arms of a Bishop, walked calmly to the window and went through the motions of blessing the people in the street. 'What are you doing?' cried the anguished wife. 'Monseigneur is performing my functions,' replied the Marquis, 'so I am performing his.'*
>
> *The crucial point about the Marquis's behaviour is that it is both unexpected and perfectly logical — but of a logic [not] usually applied to this type of situation.* The Act of Creation, *p. 96*

If that is still too much pudding proof and not enough pudding taste, how about a possibly slightly less theoretically incongruent humorous story:

A kangaroo hopped into an outback bar and asked for a beer.
  'That will be $7.50,' said the barperson.
  The kangaroo paid for the drink and drank it.
  'We don't get many kangaroos in here,' said the barperson, as the kangaroo started to hop out.
  'And that's no wonder,' replied the kangaroo, 'with the prices you charge!'

Another theory of humour is Aaron Smuts's *play theory*.[3] According to this theory, humour is a mechanism through which we humans play with each other. This function of humour might be particularly important for those of us who don't play a very non-competitive version of organized sport or sex, and have therefore officially retired from play (ie, grown up). Smuts sees humour as connecting human adults with their need to play, and with other adult animals, such as dolphins, birds, etc, who all play.

This theory of humour relates to theories of life espoused by many great human help systems (i.e. philosophies and religions) that life is merely a play, and therefore something to be *enjoyed*, and even, occasionally at least, laughed at:

... a tale/ Told by an idiot full of sound and fury,/ Signifying nothing.
William Shakespeare, Macbeth, *Act 5, Scene 5*

Another theory of humour is one that I have just invented. Humour allows us to transcend what we normally think about and react to. Humour allows us to access a deep aspect of ourselves that is not upset by our life circumstances, no matter how dire we think they are, because this aspect of ourselves is beyond what we think. If we see the joke, then we see beyond our attachments to our thoughts, and we are the consciousness that observes. Humour allows us to transcend our ego — our individual self and its limitations. When we see the funny side, it is because we transcend our perceived need to angrily defend a big idea of a small self, because we have let it go. This experience is so wonder-fully freeing that it can make us smile, or laugh, or love.

Types of humour

*Sometimes I wonder whether the world is being run by smart people who
are putting us on or by imbeciles who really mean it.* Attributed to Mark Twain

Is there one type of humour or are there different types, as there are different blood types, eye colours and, according to some theories at least, different
human and divine personality types? Does the power of humour to make us
smile, laugh and even love depend on its type, as well as its depth?
According to Smuts[3], there are three types of humour:

1   **Humour as superiority. According to this theory, humour is popular at
    least with some of us, some of the time, because it makes us feel supe-
    rior. According to this theory, we regard certain situations and stories
    as funny because they make us feel better than someone else.**

    Examples of humour as superiority include finding humour in sarcasm,
    racist jokes, and situations that make us feel better than other people or
    groups of people. These situations include ordinary practical jokes, and
    also self-inflicted practical jokes, such as when someone slips on a banana
    skin, or falls off a chair, or makes an outrageous gaffe in school or in par-
    liament.
        Humour as superiority is not a particularly high-minded form of
    humour, and is especially popular in juvenile and aggressive environments,
    such as schools, jails and parliaments.

2   **Humour as relief. According to this theory, humour allows us to let off
    steam. This type of humour was apparently particularly popular when
    people were particularly socially repressed, such as at the cusp of the
    nineteenth and twentieth centuries.**

    An example of humour as relief is Carl Jung's response to the persua-
    sive power and passion of Sigmund Freud's sexual symbolism theories:
    'Sometimes a cigar is just a smoke!'

Another example of comic or cosmic relief is:

A man decided that he badly needed to join a monastery. He joined a monastic order in which the inhabitants were allowed to say only two words a year.

After his first year the man said his first two words to the head monk: 'More food!'

After his second year he said: 'More blankets!'

After his third year he said: 'I quit!'

The head monk replied: 'Good. You've done nothing but complain ever since you arrived here!'

Humour as relief is a higher form of humour than humour as superiority, because it isn't used to puff up our own ego at the expense of someone else's ego — it's not divisive.

3   **Humour as incongruence.** This theory of humour has been propounded by such great humour experts, if not necessarily great humourists, as Professor Immanuel Kant and Aristotle. According to this theory, humour is funny because it involves situations that are incongruent with what we would expect in these situations.

An example of humour as incongruence is a story that was told in Germany about an autobahn phenomenon known as ghost drivers. A ghost driver is a driver who drives the wrong way up an autobahn — not for very long. One day a warning blared onto a driver's radio:

'Beware, there is a ghost driver on the autobahn!'

'Ghost driver!' responded the driver. 'There isn't a ghost driver, there are hundreds of them!'

The driver was the ghost driver!

This is a higher form of humour than humour as superiority, because it leads to an expansion of our usual perceptions. The incongruence of incongruent

humour lies in its sudden shift: the jolt that it gives to our usual way of perceiving. We assume that something is 'normal' in an incongruently humorous story; in this case, that our autobahn driver is a regular driver. Then we are surprised and delighted to discover that we had it all wrong — our regular autobahn driver is actually the ghost driver!

An example of a story that has elements of all three of the above types of humour, and perhaps therefore unifies them, is:

> *An Englishman a Frenchman and a Russian are having a drink together in*
> *a bar, when the topic of happiness comes up.*
>   *'Happiness,' says the Englishman, 'is when you are sitting at home on a*
> *cold night in front of a good fire, with a nice cup of tea and a crumpet.'*
>   *'You English are so unromantic!' the Frenchman responded.*
> *'Happiness is when you are having an affair with a beautiful woman and*
> *no one finds out!'*
>   *'You are both wrong,' said the Russian. 'Happiness is when someone*
> *bangs on your door at three o'clock in the morning and says "Ivan*
> *Skabinski, come out!", and you can say "Ivan Skabinski lives next door!" '*

Can getting a joke be the same as getting reminded or heartened or enlightened by realising that our life means something completely different to what we thought it meant? Rather than thinking too much about what humour is and what types of humour there are, and not just enjoying it, we could simply divide humour into:

- **humour that hurts people, because it is based on and reinforces what separates us, and**
- **humour that helps people, because it is based on and reinforces what brings us together.**

Humour can contract our natural heartfulness, and it can expand it. What's the difference?

Humour and heartfulness

Humor must not professedly teach, and it must not professedly preach, but it must do both if it would live forever. Mark Twain

Whether humour expands or contracts our heartfulness depends on what we use it for. When we open our hearts and our minds and our lives to our natural good humour, we can see that nothing is so deadly or so serious that it can't make us smile or even laugh, even if it is at ourselves.

Using humour to take ourselves less seriously

If I had no sense of humour, I would long ago have committed suicide. Mahatma Gandhi

When we use humour to smile or even laugh at ourselves, we transcend our small, reactive, threatened and miserable selves, even if we think that we have something to be small, reactive, threatened and miserable about. When we feel like defending ourselves, or attacking someone else, or blaming someone else, or rationalising, or getting upset, and we instead feel happy and humorous because we have seen a joke rather than a disaster, then we are free. If we don't blindly react to a trivial life event, such as a perceived insult, as we always react, mechanically and defensively, then we haven't allowed whatever has happened to rob us of our happiness. If we see irony rather than insult, we are free to create a new way of responding to our life events, one which helps us and other people stay happy and connected.

Khrushchev the comedian
Nikita Khrushchev is probably better remembered as a former leader of the Soviet Union than as a comedian and diffusor of potentially highly damaging tensions; however, he actually played all three of these highly compatible roles. Those of us who remember Nikita Khrushchev, or have read about him, might best remember the publicly highly antagonistic role

he played with American president John F Kennedy during the Cuban missile crisis of 1963, which could have led to nuclear war. There was much more, however, to this crisis and to Nikita Khrushchev than most historical accounts recall, and this included his real secret weapon: his ability to laugh at himself.

At a crowded and important Soviet leaders meeting, Nikita Khrushchev heard a voice ask: 'Why didn't you oppose Josef Stalin and his atrocities?'

'Who said that?' Khrushchev thundered.

There was total silence.

'That's why I didn't oppose Josef Stalin!'

At another important Soviet meeting, Nikita Khrushchev heard someone call him a fool: 'Twenty years in the Gulag for treason!' Khrushchev thundered. 'And another 20 years for revealing a state secret!'

There have been plenty of world leaders, business leaders and family leaders who haven't been able to laugh at themselves, even when they knew they were laughably wrong. This is because their ego was too tightly inflated for them to diffuse pressure on themselves and others by admitting that they were wrong. You might even be able to think of examples of people who would greatly benefit greatly from being able to open their minds, their hearts and their heartfulness by letting go of their serious and seriously damaging ideas of themselves by letting the light and the lightness in.

Using humour to lighten our life load

The play's the thing ...
William Shakespeare, Hamlet, Act 2, Scene 2

All the world's a stage,
And all the men and women merely players;
They have their exits and their entrances,
And one man in his time plays many parts.
William Shakespeare, As You Like It, Act 2, Scene 7

This world [is] like a stage
Whereon many play their parts; the lookers-on, the sage …
Pythagoras

Humour helps us let go of our life load by connecting us with our life play. Humour helps us let go of what is getting in the way of our play, by allowing us to let go of our ideas, our habits, our biases, our misery, and connect with the opportunity to live a whole life as well as play a life part.

So how do we let go?

It might seem impossible to let go of a heavy physical object, such as a suitcase full of stuff that we have been carrying around for a long time, just because we have been carrying it around for a long time. But is it?

It might seem impossible to let go of a heavy mental object, such as a wrong belief about ourselves or someone else that we have been carrying around for a long time, just because we have been carrying it around for a long time. But is it?

It might seem impossible to let go of a heavy emotional object, such as an accusation or a grudge that we have been carrying around for a long time, just because we have been carrying it around for a long time. But is it?

The best way to let go of anything is to see that we are carrying something heavy that we don't need — a burden. The next step is realising that we don't need it. The third step is to find the light and the lightness by dropping the heaviness.

The benefits of humour

Humour is by far the most significant activity of the human brain. Edward de Bono

Humor is an antidote to all ills. Patch Adams

There is a popular understanding of the scientific research literature that is not always congruent with the scientific understanding of the scientific research literature. There is a popular idea, for example, that adults smile less often than young children do. This may well be true; however, there is no strong

scientific evidence of it being true. There is, however, strong scientific evidence that adults smile less often in public than children do, which says something interesting about what happens when we grow up, and what we can lose. Chappell and Temple[4] conducted a study of 15,824 children, adolescents, young adults, middle-aged adults and older adults, which showed a decrease across age groups in public smiling. They attributed this to an increase over time in 'emotional regulation'. What this might really mean is that we adults feel a growing need to take ourselves seriously, to be 'adults'. Given the scientifically demonstrated and obvious common-sense benefits of humour for us and for our heartfulness, this is so sad that it's funny!

Smiling frequently is our natural state, as is laughing, as is good humour. Realising our natural heartfulness protects and strengthens our natural good humour, and realising our natural good humour protects and strengthens our natural heartfulness. Humour and laughter can keep us in a good place and space, and they can help us return to it. Humour and laughter are the natural antidote to our stress and even to our emotional and physical pain because of their vital benefits, including the following:

- *Medical benefits:* Humour releases endorphins (our body's natural painkillers), and boosts our immune system by increasing the level of T cells and lowering cortisol levels. Wilkins and Eisenbraun[5] found that it doesn't matter which of the three main types of humour described above we use, because they all lead to important physiological benefits.

- *Psychological benefits:* Humour promotes a positive outlook, and helps us cope with difficult situations. Cann and Collette[6] found that humour helps us reappraise threats, builds strength of character, and facilitates happiness. They also found that humour can help us globally as well as individually, by helping us all maintain 'more stable positive affect'.

- *Heartful benefits:* Humour helps us connect, with other people and with ourselves, which is the best way to develop and maintain happiness.

The power of humour to deeply help us and even to deeply heal us — by healing something deeper than our physical and psychological maladies — is recognized by programmes such as Clown Care[7, 8] and by laughter-therapy groups.

Clown Care is a programme that operates in hospitals and medical centres around the world, and involves visits from specially trained clowns, sometimes called 'Clown doctors', which is a trademarked name in some countries. These emergency light-relief sessions have been shown to help heal patients with the positive power of hope and humour.

Clown doctors started working in hospitals in New York in 1986 under a programme called the Big Apple Circus Clown Care Unit, which started by Michael Christensen, and now operate all over the United States, Canada, Europe, Australia and Israel. The movie *Patch Adams*, about a well-known and successful clown doctor, heightened international awareness of this programme.

Clown Care is mainly aimed at helping children cope with the mysteries, discomforts and stresses of being hospitalized, by parodying and lightening the hospital routine. In some countries, it also helps adults. It is even possible that the active ingredient of the clown doctor approach to lightening our life loads in hospitals could be successfully transplanted into other institutions that can be mysterious, uncomfortable and stressful, such as our workplaces and homes.

Laughter groups began in Mumbai in the early 1990s as a form of laughter yoga, when an Indian medical doctor, Dr Madan Kataria, was studying the medical benefits of laughter, and decided to put his research into practice. Laughter groups typically consist of people coming together under the care of a lead laugher, who uses various stratagems to help their groups forget their seriousness and just start laughing — it doesn't matter how or what about. There are even corporate laughter consultants who increase staff morale, wellbeing, creativity and productivity just by helping workers to let go of whatever is stopping them from seeing the lightness.

Humour in action

- See life as a play. Life has been described by such highly varied human truth systems as the Hindu religion and stand-up comedy as something that seems much worse than it really is, and much more serious than it really is. According to Hinduism, life is a divine dance, between the divine player Krishna and his divine leading lady, Leela. According to stand-up comedy, life is always darkest before the dawn — of the punchline.

- Help other people find the light and the lightness by finding it yourself. Often the person who sees the humour in a situation is the person who is transcending the situation, and is the person whom other people will follow.

- Acknowledge that life isn't as deadly or as serious as it sometimes seems. Do something light and lightening every day to remind yourself!

- Observe humour and how having ready access to it can help open us up to our great life opportunities —such as by reading about it, or by observing it in a great life teacher, such as a great clown or a young child ... or yourself.

TAKE-HOME TIPS

- Being light is the best way of seeing the light.

- Don't wait for something to smile about, smile!

- Don't wait for someone else to laugh before you laugh — just laugh!

- Don't wait until things are disastrously serious before you see the funny side.

- If you can't see anything to smile at or laugh at, keep looking.

- See the joke and see the hope.

- Enjoy the show!

Examples of the good-humoured path to heartfulness

Sometimes our lives, like our jokes, are most revealing in their endings. Maybe humour is most powerful and most heartful when we need it most. Here are some true examples of people managing to see lightness in themselves and in their life situation when nothing else mattered. It has been said that if we go through most of our lives without being enlightened, there is no need for us to worry, because if we couldn't find anything in our lives to inspire enlightenment, we can find something at the end of our lives to inspire it. Maybe it is the same with humour. Here is a selection of 'famous last words':

Humour as our final solution

I told you I was ill.
Inscription on Spike Milligan's gravestone

Either that wallpaper goes, or I do.
Oscar Wilde's last words

When the French philosopher Voltaire was asked on his deathbed to renounce Satan, he replied, 'This is no time to make new enemies.'

On his way to be beheaded, England's King Charles the First was asked whether he would like a whiskey. 'Yes,' he replied, 'and you might make it a double!' He then said of his fate: 'It is a harsh medicine, but it cures all ills.' I told my future wife this story at our wedding rehearsal ...

Die, my dear? Why that's the last thing I'll do!
Groucho Marx

Go on, get out! Last words are for fools who haven't said enough!
Karl Marx (when asked by his housekeeper for his last words)

Time is a great teacher, but unfortunately it kills all its pupils.
Victor Berlioz

The humour bottomless line

We automatically let go of our excess life baggage when we lighten our minds and our hearts, and we do this by opening our minds and our hearts to let our whole lives in. We automatically transform darkness into light when we open our eyes. When our eyes are open, it is easy to open our minds and our hearts and our entire lives, because we can see that we need to, and that we can. How?

We may think that we have no time for humour, or that we can't afford it, or we:

- are too busy
- have better things to do
- are too important/unimportant
- don't need it, or
- don't need it now.

Do we have time for love? There is a relationship between love and laughter, including the connecting fact that we don't really need either of them, if our need is defined by a board of directors or a stressed mind. We need love because it makes our life better. We need humour for the same reason. We can fulfil our need for humour the same way that we can fulfil our need for love, by opening up to it.

We can find heartfulness through humour, and we can find humour through heartfulness, simply by realising that good humour isn't a distraction from life, it *is* life. The even better news is that we already have humour, no matter what we think — we might just need to rediscover its path. When we fully allow life by being fully aware of it and fully accepting of it, we connect with our deep selves and other people's deep selves. Humour can take us to and from this eternally happy place.

References and further reading

1   http://www.etymonline.com/index.php?term=wit

2   Koestler, A. (1964). *The Act of Creation*. Hutchinson, London.

3   Smuts, A. 'Humor'. *Internet Encyclopedia of Philosophy*.

4   Chapell, M and Temple, U. (1997). Frequency of public smiling across the life span. *Perceptual and Motor Skills*, 85(3, Pt 2): 1326.

5   Wilkins, J and Eisenbraun, A. (2009). Humor theories and the physiological benefits of laughter. *Advances in Mind-Body Medicine*, 24(2): 8–12.

6   Cann, A and Collette, C. (2014). Sense of humor, stable affect, and psychological well-being. *Europe's Journal of Psychology*, 10(3): 464–479.

7   Wojciechowski, M. (2007). Tickling the funny bone: the use and benefits of humor in health care. *PT: Magazine of Physical Therapy*, 15(12): 20–25.

8.   Spitzer, P. (2001). The clown doctors. *Australian Family Physician*, 30(1): 12–16, 53–55.

CHAPTER 8

Contentment

*Whatever we are waiting for — peace of mind,
contentment, grace, the inner awareness of simple
abundance — it will surely come to us, but only
when we are ready to receive it with an open
and grateful heart.*

Sarah Ban Breathnach

What does contentment feel like?

Are you feeling it now?

Have you ever felt it?

What does discontentment feel like?

Are you feeling it now?

Have you ever felt it?

What is the difference between contentment and discontentment?

Contentment isn't as fashionable as stress release or as sexy as enlightenment. How many company CEOs report that their company's contentment has gone up over the past financial year? How many self-help book readers or self-development course participants want to be more content at the end of their book or course than they were at the start of it? How many workers are working their way towards contentment? How many schools teach contentment? How many children tell you that they want to be content when they grow up?

We get life's great irony and opportunity when we realize that when we are content with what we have, we have it all. When we stop looking *out there* for life and love and reasons to love life, we realize that we have it all *in here*, and always did, and always will.

The ex-messiah Jiddu Krishnamurti once started a talk to a large audience in India by promising to give them the secret of happiness at the end of the talk. There haven't been many ex-messiahs, which makes Jiddu Krishnamurti and his secrets even more special. Jiddu Krishnamurti was an otherwize relatively ordinary southern Indian boy who was 'discovered' in the early twentieth century as a modern messiah. This 'discovery' was by Annie Besant, the second President of the Theosophical Society, an organisation that continues to seek to bring together philosophy and religion as complementary paths to a common life truth. In 1912 Krishnamurti retired as a messiah at the age of seventeen, and was content to spend his next 74 years as an ordinary great sage, writer, speaker, teacher and life knowledge expert.

Promising to give the secret of happiness at the end of a talk is a great way of encouraging an audience to stay. We can do the same thing in this chapter on contentment, because it's the same secret.

What is contentment?

The world is full of people looking for spectacular happiness while they snub contentment. Doug Larson

What is contentment, and how do we get it, soon? The Oxford online dictionary defines contentment as 'a state of peaceful happiness'. Are you content with that explanation, or would you like something more? The Oxford online dictionary also tells us that the word 'content' is one of the top thousand most frequently used English words. Does this mean that there is a lot of contentment out there, or a lot of talk about it, or what?

Is contentment absolute or is it in the 'I' of its beholder?

What causes contentment, and its opposite?

What's in contentment for me?

The answers to these questions and more may be revealed below, if you are content to wait ...

Charles Dickens's Mr Micawber was based on Dickens's own father, and Micawber sagely observes in *David Copperfield* that:

Annual income twenty pounds, annual expenditure nineteen and six, result happiness. Annual income twenty pounds, annual expenditure twenty pounds nought and six, result misery.

Wanting what we don't have is what motivates discontented people to be discontented. This is what motivates debtors to keep running up debts, and gamblers to keep gambling, and alcoholics to keep drinking, and workaholics to

keep working, and shopaholics to keep shopping, and donkeys to keep plodding along after carrots held out in front of them by a stick — always. Wanting what we don't have is what motivates children who think they will get what they want when they grow up, and grown-ups who think they had what they wanted when they were children. Wanting what we don't have is the source of all our discontents, because we can only be content, we can only be happy, with what we already have — right here and right now.

Contentment and the ongoing happiness that it allows is the opposite of desire and the ongoing unhappiness that it causes. Chronic desire is craving, and extreme desire is addiction. Addiction can be seen as a dis-ease, and it is even more common than what we think it is. Clinical or official addictions, such as to alcohol or other drugs, are only the tip of the addiction iceberg. Most of our addictions are *unofficial*, such as to over-eating, or to working too hard, or to success, or to getting our own way, or to worrying about what people think of us, or to the future or to … thinking. Any compulsive desire for something that we don't have or are not experiencing here and now is an addiction, and this is the opposite of contentment.

Contentment and heartfulness

I don't look for bliss, just contentment. Alison Krauss

When we are heartful we can finally stop looking out for happiness and contentment, because when we are heartful we have found them, deep inside us. When we stop looking out, we are heartful, because we have arrived at the start and the end of our journey to the centre of our being. When we are heartful, we don't need to look for anything because we have found everything — in the last place we would think to look for it: in ourselves.

When we are content, we are automatically mindful because we are fully aware and fully accepting of what we are experiencing. When we are content, we are also more than what mindful has come to mean, because we are aware and accepting of more than our experiences; we are aware and accepting of the source of our experiences. When we are content, we are whole, and therefore not addicted to any need for more than what we have or are. When we are content, we are no longer searching, because we have arrived.

When we are heartful we are automatically content with whatever is happening inside us — our thoughts, our bodily sensations, our emotions. We are also content with our disguized emotions — our thoughts and our bodily sensations. When we are heartful, we are even content with our discontentment, because we are no longer the victims of our story, we are its creators. When we are heartful, we are automatically content with whatever is happening outside us, because when we are heartful we realize that nothing is happening outside us.

Contentment isn't fashionable or sexy for the same reason that heartfulness isn't fashionable or sexy yet, because fashion and sexiness are based on our placing an artificial value on *change*. What is real doesn't change, and therefore can't go out of fashion or supply, and it therefore doesn't make anyone any money. If we were content to value our contentment, if we took our heartfulness to heart, we would have all we need, and we wouldn't need to be addicted to need.

When we are content to be open-hearted, as well as open-minded, we realize that we don't need to solve the mystery of life, the universe and everything, because we *are* the mystery of life, the universe and everything. So where do we start?

The gratitude attitude

Acceptance leads us to love, gratitude leads us to contentment.

In a world that can look as though it lacks love and contentment, what do we have to be grateful for? A funny thing about humour is that the more we find to laugh at, the funnier life gets. It's the same with gratitude. The more we find to be grateful for, the more generous life gets. When we keep looking for what we are owed or for what we should have or could have, we can lose our natural gratitude attitude.

Gratitude allows us to fully connect and to fully care about what we are connected to, and this allows us to be content with everything — whatever is happening right here, right now. Gratitude is the opposite of discontentment,

and the opposite of craving, and the opposite of addiction, because it allows us to find our infinite life value by recognising that our present life is a gift. When we are thankful for our part in our life script, whatever it is, we will play it well, and we will help other people play their parts well. Gratitude and its heartfelt rewards begin with a simple choice: between resenting what I am not and valuing what I am.

The great life instruction manuals known as children's stories give us powerfully practical life lessons about the power of gratitude to make us content, and the power of contentment to make us heartful, and the power of heartfulness to make us happy:

> *We are all ugly ducklings. We all suffer when we think that we are bad ducks or bad anything else's because such thoughts are destructively wrong. We can instead be grateful at any moment and at every moment for being beautiful swans, because we are all something much more beautiful than what we think we are.*

The great life instruction manuals known as adults' stories, philosophies, religions, psychology and irony also give us powerfully practical life lessons about the power of gratitude.

There is a Buddhist story about a turtle that is really a story about our having much more to be grateful for/ content with/ heartful in than what we think we have. There are similar stories in other life knowledge traditions, about other life forms, because it is all the same story …

> *Picture in your mind a blind turtle swimming in a large sea. An oxen yoke is drifting on top of the sea, and, as the turtle surfaces to breathe, it sticks its head into the yoke … Your chance of being born as a human being was less than that turtle had of surfacing into the yoke … You are that fortunate!*

Gestalt perceptual psychologists, cognitive-behavioural clinical psychologists, and whodunit writers all make the telling point that it is not what is out there that really matters, it is what we see. We might feel resentful because our life or our wife or husband or job or dog or whatever seems worse than someone else's, or worse than what we 'should' have, or worse than they were. There are times when it is more accurate as well as kind, however, to be grateful for what we have, rather than resentful of what we haven't.

> *It is nobler as well as nicer to be grateful that we still have a leg to stand on, than to be resentful that our argument doesn't have a leg to stand on.*

There are common sayings that, like many common things, are lessons in the power of gratitude:

> *Blind Freddie would be glad to see it!*
> *Worse things happen at sea!*

The essence of these sayings is that no matter how bad things seem they could be worse, or rather there is always something to be grateful for as long as we live, as long as someone we love lives, as long as there is life and love. The best and only time to be grateful for what we have, and not resentful for what we haven't, is while we have it, which means *now*.

Realising that our present is a gift

I often sang my daughter Miranda songs before she could talk. As soon as she could talk, she asked me to stop. She still lets me sing her one song, however; a 1970s song which is actually a much older traditional African song, 'The Lion Sleeps Tonight'. The sleeping lion symbolizes death, which sleeps for as long as we don't sleep, when we are awake in our eternal living moment.

A key to mindfulness is being content with the gift of the present. A key to heartfulness is accepting our whole life gift, strings and all. When we are heartful we live in the moment and we live in it deeply, which means we are fully aware of what we have, fully accepting of it, fully focused on it and fully caring about it, and whoever gave it to us.

Living heartfully means accepting the gift of our connection with every-thing, even with the fleeting, because sometimes we don't realize the infinitely

large until we realize the infinitely small.

Living heartfully means realising that life is a process not a structure, and a question and not an answer.

Living heartfully means allowing life to flow eternally free and undammed.

Benefits of contentment

Contentment does not come from achievement. Paul Henderson

Is our greatest life experience just doing whatever we are doing right here and now, such as reading this book, and being content with it?

A large scientific study at Harvard University showed that simply giving our full attention to what we are doing right here and right now — being content with the reality of what is — makes us happiest.[1] Are you content with this benefit of contentment, or would you like more?

Contentment in action

There is a wonderful ancient American Indian story about contentment in action:

> *Two wolves are wrestling, in my mind. One wolf is ravenous and destructive and wants only to destroy. The other wolf is noble and kind. Which one will triumph?*
> *The one that I feed.*

There is a wonderful ancient Asian Indian story of contentment in action:

> *What we give our attention to grows.*

- **If we feed our discontentment with our attention, it will grow stronger, until it grows into anger, and then**

destruction. If we feed our contentment with our attention, it will grow stronger, into peace and then happiness.

- We can start practising contentment right now by being grateful right now, for what and who we have. We might need some preliminary open-heartfulness surgery before we can pull this off permanently. We can start this by re-modelling our thought forms, such as by realising that what and who we have is actually always exactly halfway between what we think is better than what we have, and what we think is worse. We can be content in the knowledge that we are actually living in perfect balance between what could be better and what could be worse, between our past and our future, and between me and you.

- Contentment comes from connection, with our source. The bridge between our inner source and its outer expression is the connection between our mind, body and essence. We renew this connection when we feel content with our lives by feeling our bodily sensations, and by being content with them.

- Contentment arises naturally when we don't try to change or control other people or ourselves. This is like trying to or kick our way out of a sandstorm or think our way out of a thought storm ... Just allow what's deep within to be, and anything that needs to change will.

- Be content to let the unhappiness buck stop with you. Make a unilateral decision to stop blindly reacting to what seems to be going wrong with your life by making life worse for other people. Just as it usually takes more than one car driver to cause a car accident, it usually takes more than one non-heartful life operator to cause a happiness accident. Be what you would really like to be.

- Realize that when you are discontented it is not really with the state of your life circumstances, it is really with the state of your life consciousness. When you are discontented you don't to have to change anything, just change the way you look at things. You don't need to go anywhere else or be anything else, just be who and where you are, more deeply.

TAKE-HOME TIPS

- Contentment starts here, and now, and with you.
- Don't try to find contentment in your life circumstances, find it in your life.
- Don't try to find contentment in your thoughts or your emotions, find it in your essence.
- Don't try to find contentment in an idea of yourself, find it in your self.
- Find contentment in what you are doing and who you are doing it with right here and right now — there is nothing else.
- No self, no worries!
- Just be ... content.

Examples of the contented path to heartfulness

There are plenty of great 'fictional' stories about the power of contentment to lead us to heartfulness, and the power of heartfulness to lead us to contentment. Here are some of my favourites:

CONTENT TO BE HOME ...

I Had Trouble Getting to Solla Sollew by Dr Seuss is, to me, a parody of the search for enlightenment, before the search for enlightenment was popular enough to need to be parodied. In this story, the hero (of typically indeterminate species or gender) has heard about a place where no one has problems, or at least very few; a wonderful place called Solla Sollew. The hero therefore leaves their problems behind and strikes out for the Promised Land. Getting to the land of no problems the hero encounters all kinds of problems, however they eventually find it ... only to find that it is locked ... The great lesson here is that the door is always locked when it is not our own door.

content to be Home or away

In Douglas Adams's *Restaurant At the End of the Universe*, Zaphod Beeblebrox is just a regular double-headed cool and ostentatious President of the Universe. The universe is really ruled, however, by someone who lives a totally simple life, who gets up every day in a simple house on a simple planet and does much the same things, including making some simple decisions about how the universe needs to proceed. The real ruler of the universe enjoys everything that happens in his simple life, including his simple decisions, because he experiences them as if for the first time, and is therefore fully content with them.

There are also many great even-truer-than-fictional stories about the heartful power of contentment. Here are some of my favourites:

content to be a great theoretical physicist ...

Stephen Hawking is no ordinary great theoretical physicist. Stephen Hawking is an exceptional great theoretical physicist, because he has an exceptional ability to make the complex real, and really interesting. We often think that people must be clever because they say things that we don't understand; however, it takes real cleverness to understand things well enough to understand their simplicity, and to explain it to the people who don't understand it, yet. Stephen Hawking has explained time and timelessness to us, and the almost infinitely large (classical physics), and the almost infinitely small (quantum mechanics). He isn't just content with being a great theoretical physicist; he is content with his life. Having a serious and seriously physically incapacitating illness, which has resulted in his spending many years in a wheelchair, and

left him only able to talk through a speech synthesizer, has not led him to resentment, or bitterness, or anger, or blame, or despair; it has led him to contentment: 'How could I have asked for more?'

content to be a great teacher ...

My maternal grandmother, Binnie, topped Australia in the then national and competitive teacher training examinations. My grandmother was invited to choose any school, anywhere, to teach in, and she chose a small school in a small town called Orbost, where her future husband and my grandfather, Phil, had been posted to. My grandmother and grandfather were totally content with her decision and with their lives.

content to be a great human being ...

My 82-year-old father, Graham, who is sitting beside me as I write, recently had a serious fall. This led to his spending seven weeks in hospital with a badly broken hip, a shattered right shoulder which can't be fixed because the operation would probably be fatal, and new, constant and serious pain and immobility. This was on top of a serious stroke almost 20 years ago that finished his career as a hospital pharmacist and left him unable to clearly produce or understand speech. This, in turn, was on top of advanced, painful and debilitating bladder cancer. There are times when my father seems frustrated and unhappy, and yet I always see something deeper than such times in him: a deep contentment with what he has, which means that he has it all. My father is fuelled by gratitude for his wife, Rita, and for his life. When I see him I feel great compassion; I also feel greatness.

The contentment bottomless line

Contentment begins at home, no matter where you live, or who with.

We get contentment in the same way that we get heartfulness: by not getting it, but by giving it, and living it. When we are content to just be, we are not has-beens or wanna-bes, we are human beings. When we are content with all that is, or isn't; when we are content with life the opportunity rather than life the big deal, we have real contentment and real life.

As we learned at the beginning of this chapter, the ex-messiah Jiddu Krishnamurti once started a talk to a large audience in India by promising to give them the secret of happiness at the end of the talk. The secret of happiness and the secret of contentment are the same, and here it is: *I don't mind what happens!*

References and further reading

1   Killingsworth, MA and Gilbert, DT. (2010). 'A wandering mind is an unhappy mind.' *Science*, 330(6006): 932. DOI: 10.1126/*science*.1192439

CHAPTER 9

Love

Love alters not with his brief hours and weeks,
But bears it out even to the edge of doom.

William Shakespeare, Sonnet 116

There is a candle in your heart, ready to be kindled. There is
a void in your soul, ready to be filled. You feel it, don't you?

Rumi, There is a Candle in Your Heart

Life is a journey to and from love.
Let it flow.

Do you have enough love?

Is love real?

Is love only real for people who have enough of it,
or enough access to it?

Is food only real for people who have enough of it,
or enough access to it?

Can you feel love so deeply that you live in it,
rather than it living in you?

What if your world seems so small that there is no room for love in it, or that there isn't even enough room for anyone else in it, or not even enough room for you in it?

What if you feel like someone or something has sucked out your life love and all that is left is a loveless fearful shell?

What if love only seems real in songs and movies and in other people's lives?

The bad news is that we all have times when it seems as though we have lost love or forgotten it, or that love has lost or forgotten us. The good news is that we don't even need to be told that such thoughts or feelings are not true. Somewhere very deep inside us we know what light is, even when we are experiencing darkness, and we know what love is, even when we are experiencing fear or despair. No matter what is happening on the outside of our lives, there is always a source of light and of love deep inside our lives. This glimmering light and love dawns deep within us when it dawns on us that our ideas about love or its lack are just ideas.

Love itself is not an idea; it is our ultimate reality. We can't really lose love and it can't really lose us, because love and life are essentially linked.

The founder of Transcendental Meditation, the Maharishi Mahesh Yogi, said: *Love is the glue that holds the universe together.* The bestselling author of *The Power of Now* and *A New Earth*, Eckhart Tolle, said that love is beyond our personal and limited experience of life, it belongs to and is a link to our

universal life. There have been numerous songs about love, too; mainly pro. The Beatles, for example, told us that love is all we need, and Leonard Cohen told us that love is our only engine of survival, as well as that there ain't no cure for it!

Love might seem precious like a diamond: rare and losable and needing to be strived for, and, if found, guarded and admired and sang and sonneted about. However, love is actually precious like the sunrise and the sunset — every-where and for everyone. We always have love because we are always in love, no matter what we think.

Love is our essential eternal being: the heart and soul of the universe and our seemingly individual bit of it. Our worst life mistake is thinking that we have lost love, when we have really just lost access to it because our minds have lost contact with what's deeper than our minds — our hearts and our collective heart. It is better to lose our minds than to lose heart, because when we lose what we think is important we gain what is really important.

We can't lose love, but we can forget where we left it. We can do this when we are confused by thinking that a drop of the love ocean is love, and therefore want it so badly that we forget that it is just a drop in the ocean. This mind-made illusion might manifest in despair about a relationship that we have lost, for whatever reason, or in anxiety or frustration with our inability to form or maintain a good relationship. That's the bad news. The good news is that we never actually lose love, just as we never actually lose heart or lose the sun on a cloudy day — we just lose sight of it.

How, then, can we re-discover pure love? How can we allow love to take us to an expanded state of connection and aliveness — heartfulness? How can heartfulness help us re-discover pure love?

What is love?

This is love: to fly toward a secret sky, to cause a hundred veils to fall each moment. First to let go of life. Finally, to take a step without feet.
Rumi, Diwan-e Shams-e Tabriz-I (The Works of Shams of Tabriz)

This is a question that is notoriously difficult to answer, without singing. We

all know what love is; we just need to remember it by forgetting what it isn't — our ideas about it, such as that it is limited to a particular person or activity. If we only had love when we were doing something we think we love, or doing something with someone we think we love, then we would be loveless most of the time.

The first definition of love given in the Oxford online dictionary is 'a strong feeling of affection'. Does this description of love help you understand it, or feel it?

The Oxford online dictionary also tells us that love is one of our thousand most frequently used words, which is a relief, especially as 'hate' isn't another one of them ... We all talk about love, and read about it, and listen to songs about it, and think about it, and even, at least occasionally, experience it — but do we know it?

The wisest man in ancient Athens, the great ancient Greek philosopher Socrates, had a lot to say about love, as well as a lot to say about many other vital things, and he saw love as he saw everything else — uniquely. In Plato's *Symposium* dialogue, Socrates was at a party where the guests talked about something even more important and entertaining than sport or sex, they talked about love. When it was Socrates' turn to speak, he told the other guests what one of his teachers, the wisest woman in Athens — Diotima — had told him about love. It is our link between the human and the divine.

The great twentieth-century Indian spiritual teacher Mata Nirmala Devi described a Universal Love, whose characteristics she described as *collectivity*. This doesn't mean sticking together; it means that wherever we are, we are connected. Mata Nirmala Devi developed a method that she called *Sahaja yoga* for expanding our Universal life/love energy, which is called *kundalini* in her tradition. This deep love/life energy is called *Ruh* in the Islamic life/love expansion tradition, and the *Holy Ghost* in the Christian life/love expansion tradition.

No matter what we think about it, love is an enormously powerful force. As with many enormous forces, such as gravity, love can be hard to see and even harder to recognize. We all know that love is an enormously powerful force; however, we might not always recognize it as a consistently powerfully positive force. Maybe whether love is always positive or not depends on what we mean by love.

There is the slippery love that we are always afraid of losing. There is also the sticky love that sticks to us like glue because it is glue, holding our universe together … What's the difference? We will explore this in the next section.

The vital thing to remember about love is that it is vital, and that it is vital for us to remember it. We also need to remember how to handle and harness a force that can be as gentle as a caress and as loud as a storm. Realising the power of love can be like picking up a thistle or riding a wild horse: it can feel like it is stinging us or breaking us if we don't know how to handle it, or it can enliven and amaze us, if we open our hearts to it.

We might think that we can make love, but actually we can't, because, no matter what we think about it, love already is. What we can do in our most honest and courageous moment is consciously return to love, or realize that we never really left it. This isn't what happens in our modern myths that helps create our modern culture, such as our movies, because they have a vested interest in people watching them and believing in them; they sell more tickets by selling a myth of love as dramatic, dark and complicated. Actually even in the movies there are glimpses of what love really is — constant, light and simple — because what is real and true is real and true everywhere. In the 1960s science fiction classic *Barberella* a beautiful male angel responded to Jane Fonda's powerful pick-up line with: 'An angel doesn't make love, an angel is love.' Maybe we are all angels, even when we are Hell's Angels.

In movies we say 'I do' when we promise to love each other until death do us part, and the memory of such a vow might be rather unhelpful, or downright miserable, when we look back at it in the context of the new and hidden faults of the person we said 'I do' to. The real-life matrimonial line is actually 'I *will*', and that phrase is the key to our lost love access. We don't really do anything, least of all love, because we *are* everything, most of all love.

Love is everywhere, yet it doesn't just happen. We have free will and also free won't, and our will is the antidote to our won't. When we lose love, we can keep floundering around regretting its loss, or resenting those who we think took it from us. We can also remember the greater will than the willfulness that makes us think we can find something better than love, and this is the will to live, and love, and help others live and love.

Types of love

How do I love thee? Let me count the ways.
Elizabeth Barrett Browning, Sonnets from the Portuguese, XLIII

Counting the ways isn't easy, just as it isn't easy to rate the beauty of sunrises and sunsets; however, we can give it a try to see if it helps us understand what love is, and isn't.

The ancient Greek language was once almost as universal and as modern as the internet is now. A well-known example of a universal and modern-life information database written in ancient Greek is The Bible, and another example is the collected works of Plato and Socrates. As well as giving us many other life-useful wise words, ancient Greek gave us three more words for love than modern English gives us. This system might not be four times as powerful as having just one word for love, but having specific words for specific types of love might help us remember exactly what love is. It is even possible that knowing what four words for love mean can help us realize that there is really only one love, even though there are plenty of ideas about it and distortions of it. Although we can only know love as an experience, not as a word, here are the useful ancient Greek signposts that point to the love experience:

- *Philia* — friendly or brotherly/sisterly love. This is the first part of the root meaning of *philosophy:* the love of knowledge (*sophia*).
- *Éros* — passionate love. This passion doesn't just mean the passion that is inspired by an erotic painting or a marvellous meal. We can also feel *Éros* for our work, or for knowledge, which means that *philosophy* should really be called *Érorosophy*, and might even be more marketable if it was!
- *Agápe* — affection or pure love, without the intensity of *Éros*. We would be more likely to *Agápe* a pleasant painting or person than to *Éros* them!
- *Storge* — dutiful love, such as of our family or employer,

even if other forms of love aren't so naturally produced by them. Maybe it would be a good deal for us to swap some *Éros* for some *Storge*! Maybe it would be good for us to dutifully ask what we can do for love, rather than ask love what it can do for us. Love isn't always sung by angels, it can be drawn by work-horses.

In other languages, there is also more than one word for love. The great Vietnamese mindfulness exponent Thich Nhat Hanh pointed out, for example, that in Vietnamese the words *tinh* and *nghia* both mean love, in different ways. *Tinh* contains a lot of passion. *Nghia* is calmer, deeper and more solid. With *nghia* you are more willing to sacrifice to make the other person happy, and it is the result of sharing difficulties and joys over a long period of time. An example of *nghia* is given in a book that my wife, Melanie, left open by my over-heated computer one morning, *Teachings on Love:*[1]

> True love contains respect. In the Vietnamese tradition, husband and wife always respect each other as honoured guests. When you practise this, your love will last for a long time.

Incidentally, the word 'hospitality' literally means the love of strangers. Maybe when we are all hospitable to our planetary boarding-house's other guests there will be no strangers.

We can make other distinctions between types of love, such as between the type that we live for and the type that we live against. There is no such thing as destructive love, yet there is a destructive idea of love that can make it unnaturally damaging, as well as naturally nurturing.

Unconditional love

Unconditional love is just love, absolutely and always. This is the love that we are full of when we are fully alive, and it is what we miss out on when we are disconnected from being fully alive, such as when we think about what we consider is better than what we have. Unconditional love is vitally valuable, because it links us with the universe as well as with our universal essence, and could also be described as unlimited love, or pure love, or universal love, or divine love.

Unconditional love is why we live, how we live and what we live for. This is the love that inspires us to live and to live well, by treating other people as if we are vitally connected to them, not because we think that we should, but because we *feel* it. We can never lose this love because we *are* this love; however, we can mislay it or distort it.

Conditional love

Conditional love is Love Pty Ltd. This is unlimited love that we have limited, pure love that we have made impure, universal or divine love that we have made personal. Loving conditionally means that we have locked up something that was free in our hearts, and therefore turned our hearts into a jail. We do this by placing conditions or limitations or barriers on our love, such as: 'I will love you if …', 'I will love you when …', 'I don't love you anymore because …', 'I only love my family, or some of it!', 'I only love my spouse/partner/special friend for now at least!', 'I only love those in those in my circle of friends, or colleagues, or fellow shoppers or club members or cult members, or sporting team supporters, or any people at all who see something the same way I do.'

Conditional love is what we live against, and it is what causes our problems. Resentments, arguments and wars are caused by conditional love. We don't resent or attack people or countries just because we gratuitously or randomly hate them. We resent or attack people or countries because our unconditional love has been blocked by conditions or limitations. We resent or attack people or countries because we love what we think they are upsetting or threatening, and our love doesn't extend to the person or organisation or country who we see as our enemy. Ironically, our most potent resentments, arguments and wars are actually caused by love — conditional love.

The wars between Christianity Pty Ltd and Islam Pty Ltd didn't start because Christians and Muslims innately hate each other; they started because of Love Pty Ltd. The love of warring Christians is limited to Christians and the love of warring Muslims is limited to Muslims, and they have not yet been able to expand their love to the divine love that they think they fight for … Warring

Christians and Muslims hate and attack those who they see as outside their circle of love, and the same principle applies to our small and large resentments and arguments. When we love me and only me, or mine and only mine, it is easy to hate everything else.

How then can we free our real love?

Love and heartfulness

Whether or not the world made sense, one had to embrace the totality of life; the whole glorious, paradoxical mess. Tai Moses, Zooburbia

We don't need to find love just as we don't need to find heartfulness, because what is vital is never lost. Sometimes, however, we need to remember where we have lost or hidden our love keys. Remembering where we have lost or hidden our pure love starts with our remembering our connection with all of our life, with our heartfulness. If we lose heart and heartfulness we lose love, and when we lose love we lose heart and heartfulness. When we forget who we really are, all we have left is an idea of who we really aren't.

The opposite to love is fear. Like all opposites, love and fear are closely linked. Fear is a distortion of love, because if we didn't love we wouldn't fear losing love. When we develop a fear habit we forget love, because we are chronically craving something that we think is better, whether it is a better relationship, car or job. What we crave is always just out of our reach, because it is a mind-made phantom, and never a realisation of what's beyond our minds. Our problems start when we distort love by wanting something out there to fill our perceived lack of love. We will actually never find love *out there*, because it's always *in here*. The heart of anything that matters is the heart of our matter: love.

How do we find love? How do we find heartfulness? How does a fish find water? Love naturally flows and grows and opens our hearts, minds and lives when we allow it to. Love is the most profitable investment we can make, and all it costs us is the realisation that it didn't leave us, we left it. If we look at the collective sales figures of all the books, movies and songs about love, we will realize that it is something we all love, at least sometimes. To paraphrase the

words of Dean Martin's 1960s classic, *Everybody loves somebody sometimes.*
We can truthfully say 'Everybody loves something sometimes'.

All we need to do to find the spark of love that will ignite our lives is open
our hearts with the key to the love that is already in them. This love is our
essence, and all we need to do to find it is identify and overcome what is in its
way: the barriers that we think that the world has put up, which really we have
put up. The barriers that we erect in our hearts to keep our pain out actually
keep our love in. When we open our hearts to let love flow out and in, we will
really live, from our heartful source.

> *Your task is not to seek for love, but merely to seek and find all the barriers
> within yourself that you have built against it.* Rumi

What we give attention to grows, and what grows can be the flowers of love
or the strangling weeds of misery if we think that we have lost love, or that
somebody has stolen it, or whatever other barrier we put up or put up with
that limits our love.

We can start on our heartful path to love *now* by choosing acceptance rather than resentment, and then working our way up to choosing compassion
rather than criticism, and then choosing love rather than fear or hate.

If we can see that people have reasons for doing what might look like
extremely unlovely things to us, just as we have reasons for doing unlovely
things to other people, and ourselves, then we can see that there is something
deeper than damage and respond to that. A minor love-access blockage can
soon escalate into a major love road-block or even a love attack when we give
our attention to the worst in people and not the best.

If we consciously let go of our unconscious desire to change people,
including ourselves (often by beating out the badness, literally or metaphorically), then we can let go of our desire to make love, when all we need to do
is *allow* love. Being heartful means giving and receiving love from our source,
rather than getting distracted by what is happening on the surface of our lives.
When we are heartful we understand that we are all on the same side, and that
together we are a perfect love play.

We can respond heartfully to whatever and whoever happens to us if

we can respond from our essence rather than from our minds or emotions. Recognising that whatever someone has done to us was caused by whatever was done to them can make us more gracious, more loving and more heartful. This process can start with us turning the other cheek as suggested by Jesus, rather than extracting an eye for an eye as suggested by the Old Testament, and by our old and new legal, business and personal political systems. Our heartful response to life begins with a conscious choice, and this means that we can choose to recognize and live in love rather than live in fear and anger. Love, like charity, like everything else worth having, begins and ends at home.

The power of love

My vegetable love should grow
Vaster than empires, and more slow;
An hundred years should go to praise
Thine eyes, and on thy forehead gaze;
Two hundred to adore each breast,
But thirty thousand to the rest;
An age at least to every part,
And the last age should show your heart.
For, lady, you deserve this state,
Nor would I love at lower rate.
Andrew Marvell, To His Coy Mistress

What is our greatest power?

Is it our power to change Nature, such as with fire, electricity or nuclear fission?

Is it our power to accept Nature, and expand it?

Is it our power to change human nature, such as with argument, criticism, threats or seduction?

Is it our power to accept human nature, and expand it?

Is it the power of love?

The power of love isn't as obvious as the power of a nuclear explosion or even a rapid pick-up, but it is far greater. The power of love doesn't demonstrate its will by opposing or by destroying or by changing; it exerts its will by connecting and expanding. Without connection we are all just random collections of sub-atomic particles that do not together form atoms. Without connection we are all just random collections of atoms that do not together make people. Without connection we are just random collections of people who do not together make families, and societies, and friends. Without love we are always some and never all.

Plenty of forces divide us, such as dissent, rebellion and conquest. There are also counter-forces that restore us to what we truly are together, no matter how far we have strayed. The power of love to keep us together and bring us back together can be obvious and it can be subtle.

There is a love force which is as obvious and as useful as gravity. There is a love force that seems to take something away from what we value, such as our freedom. This force can be called *sacrifice*, such as when we give something away that we value, or when we are damaged by helping someone else. This only *seems* like a loss, however, because love is magical: the more of it we give away, the more of it we have. There is even a love force and source that is the force and source of life itself, which we can feel as something physical and real, such as a tingling in our bodies or a buzzing in our minds or an indescribable feeling in our hearts.

Love as a subtle energy force has many names, and it has been described in many life and love traditions. These traditions are not really different, in the same way that different brands of tuna are not really different products, and different love songs are not really about different loves. What seems to be fundamentally different can just be different entry points or signposts to the same thing. The following are some seemingly different versions of our subtle love and life energy:

- *Yoga/T'ai chi:* These are ancient Indian and Chinese versions of the same coming together — of mind, body and spirit — and are combined mental, physical and spiritual harmonising exercises.
- *Kundalini/Ruh/The Holy Ghost:* These are ancient Hindu/

Vedic, Muslim and Christian descriptions of the same extremely subtle and extremely powerful energy force. We can access this force when we are so still that we are no longer ruled by the far less subtle and far less powerful mental, emotional and physical states that habitually distract us from our true life potential.

- *The zone/flow/high creativity states:* These are 'ordinary' life equivalents of the extraordinary states described in spiritual traditions as 'spiritual' states. When we enter these states we can reveal seemingly miraculous powers that allow us to achieve great sporting, creative and other performances.

- *Miraculous healing/living:* There is scientific evidence of miracles as well as eyewitness accounts of them. The so-called placebo effect, for example, shows our ability to enter an extraordinarily powerful healing, living and loving state.

When we enter any of these subtle energy states we have no friction, no division, no waste of energy, no mistakes, no ideas, because we are pure action potential, pure knowing, pure understanding, pure being ... anything.

The benefits of love

Love is infinite, fear is small.

Despite our strong faith in modern medicine, there is actually very limited scientific evidence that supports our mass modern mind's idea that medical and psychological treatments work. Most of our medical and psychological treatments actually don't work, or rather they don't work for the reasons that those who sell them and those who buy them *think* they work.

Although things are much better than they were a generation ago, it is still the case that only about 15 percent of all contemporary clinical

interventions are supported by objective scientific evidence that they do more good than harm. On the other hand, between 40 and 60 percent of all therapeutic benefits can be attributed to a combination of placebo and Hawthorne effects, two code words for caring and concern, or what most people call 'love'.

Kerr L White, MD

Retired Deputy Director for Health Sciences

Rockefeller Foundation, USA

Although this assessment was written a generation ago, in 1988, and evidence supporting the effectiveness of many psychological and medical interventions has improved since then, there remains a great overestimation of the power of pills and a great underestimation of the power of love.

The Hawthorn effect occurs when knowledge that an experiment is taking place influences the results of the experiment, in the same way that when we observe something it can behave differently to the way that it usually behaves. The power of the placebo effect is demonstrated by people recovering from physical or psychological illness because they think that they are taking something that will make them better, even if it's a sugar pill or a non-active therapy. Scientific studies have shown that the 'treatment' success of placebo pills can even be influenced by their size and colour,[2] and that antidepressants with low side-effects don't work as well as those with high side-effect levels — 'If it hurts it must be good for me!'[3]

The power of a sugar pill to cure even serious medical problems isn't really a testament to the power of sugar, or even pills. It is a testament to the power of love that can heal people even when they don't recognize their medication's active ingredient.

An important example of a modern medical myth arising because of the power of placebo is that of antidepressants. A study by Kirch[4] found that if you include studies that don't show a benefit of antidepressants in an analysis of the results of many studies (which you need to do to be scientific and fair), then they have only been proven to be effective for severe depression, and not for moderate or mild depression. Another example is vitamins. Many of us have an unquestioning faith in the scientific value of vitamins, and yet most

synthetic (human-made) vitamins actually have no benefits, or have benefits for something other than what the people who take them think they are taking them for. Fish oil, for example, has no benefit for osteoarthritis, only for the much rarer rheumatoid arthritis.

However, many scientific studies support the power of love, sometimes described as love, sometimes described as a research rose by any other name (such as the placebo effect). For example, Abraham Maslow was a famous psychologist who devised the theory of self-actualisation: we are only truly fulfilled, only fully happy, when we are living life to our full potential, when we are playing our true part, when we know ourselves. Maslow was also interested in why and how some people who have very serious medical problems such as cancer suddenly get better, for no apparent reason, which is described medically as 'spontaneous remission'. He conducted a large study of this phenomenon and found that the people who suddenly and inexplicably became well all reported what he called peak experiences — of love. Deepak Chopra has also described the power of love to heal even very serious illnesses in *Quantum Healing*[5] and *The Path to Love*.[6]

There is substantial scientific evidence supporting the power of the placebo effect, and demonstrating that it isn't just an annoying phenomenon that makes it hard to prove that a treatment works, because it needs to work better than a placebo. The placebo effect isn't really a *no treatment* condition, it's a *no external treatment* condition. We have far more power than we think we have, because the power of our heart and our heartfulness is far greater than the power of our mind and our mindfulness.

Love in action

- Don't limit your love to particular people or groups of people, such as your immediate family or friends or work colleagues or political party or cult. Allow love to do what it does naturally: flow and grow and include — infinitely …

- Allow your love energy to flow and grow in any way you can, including by connecting with the life and love expanding approaches described above, by:

- *Yoga/T'ai chi:* Feel your deep life energy. Focus on the place and space where your mind meets your body. Be totally aware of your breath or your bodily sensations, in movement and in stillness. Allow this life and love energy to flow and grow.

- *Kundalini/Ruh/The Holy Ghost:* Allow yourself to transcend your personal and habitual nature ... Allow your impersonal/fully conscious/divine nature to express itself through you ... Be totally aware of the energy fields in your body that are automatic/universal, that may seem new or unusual or transcendent. Allow them to flow and grow and be real. Feeling this flowing, growing subtle energy can have powerful benefits — don't limit them with ideas about them.

- *The zone/flow/creativity:* Allow yourself to enter a deep state of harmony, where your performance isn't limited by competing desires or expectations ... Allow a pure expression of your deepest potential to be reflected in your deepest purpose ...

- *Miraculous healing/living:* Allow your life and love to be the miracle that it is, by getting out of its way.

- **Find your way home to love by working your way home to it in stages:**

  - *Empathy:* Realize that you are not as separate from other people as you or they might think. Find and feel something, anything, that you have in common with another person or people. This might even be the fact that we all suffer, or that we are all looking for a way out of suffering, or that we are all looking for love, or that we all living, in love.

  - *Forgiveness:* This comes naturally when we recognize that life can be as hard for other people as it is for us. We can all be blown off our life and love course by our and other people's mind-storms.

  - *Compassion:* Recognize that what we do to others we do to ourselves.

TAKE-HOME TIPS

- Don't allow your love to rust due to lack of use, or to get distorted by misuse.
- Recognize what is getting in love's way, and let it go.
- Don't wait until you feel love before you express it: do it now, mean it later.
- Don't harbour grudges, harbour love.
- Find your heartful harbour and rest in the love that you find there.
- Let go of all that isn't love.
- Meditate on love.
- Feel your heart, and your heartfulness.

Examples of the loving path to heartfulness

History is a love story. We might think that love and its opposite are modern inventions, because we might think that history consists of people doing what the history books record. Recorded history is actually just a list of events. Real history is a love story — of *why* the events happened.

> **A timeless love story**
> *This day and age we're living in*
> *Gives cause for apprehension*
> *With speed and new invention*
> *And things like third dimension.*
>
> *Yet we get a trifle weary*
> *With Mr Einstein's theory.*
> *So we must get down to earth*
> *At times relax, relieve the tension*
>
> *No matter what the progress*
> *Or what may yet be proved*
> *The simple facts of life are such*
> *They cannot be removed.*

You must remember this
A kiss is still a kiss, a sigh is just a sigh.
The fundamental things apply
As time goes by.

As Time Goes By, music and words by Herman Hupfeld, 1931
The last verse was sung by Dooley Wilson (Sam) in Casablanca, 1942

The reason why history happened as it did, and the reason why it happened, is that we have always thrown ourselves willingly into new ways of finding love — into caves, into farms, into cities, into philosophies, into religions, into medicine, into art, into science, into work, into sport, into relationships ... Sometimes we have missed. The literal translation of 'sin' is to miss the mark. Has that ever happened to you? Sometimes we aim at love and end up in arguments, feuds, wars, industrial tribunals, scientific and creative disputes, and relationship breakdowns. Our human story has always begun and ended in love, however, because if it didn't our story would be over.

Our personal history is also a love story; a trip from Heaven to Heaven, via Hell ... We can take the direct route to love, by opening ourselves to its heartful source, or we can take the scenic or screamic route by learning our love lessons the hard way. The most powerful example of a love story is *your* love story. Think of an example, any example, of you or someone you love choosing love rather than what looked like a better option. What did it mean? Has that love disappeared or does it live eternally — in your and their and our hearts?

The love bottomless line

Is life a problem or a solution?

Do I have a problem with life or do I have a life?

Is love a problem or a solution?

Do I have a problem with love or am I love?

Where is the last place you would think to look for your or someone else's lost or mislaid love? Follow your fear, or anger or frustration, or resentment, or despair or whatever all the way to a place of space. Rest in this space and allow it to *replace* your fear, or anger or despair or whatever with love.

How can we find the love that will take us to our heartfulness, or the heartfulness that will take us to our love? We can't, because we already have it. We can't, because we already are it. We can *be* love when we get out of our way. Go well, be well, be always.

References and further reading

1 Thich Nhat Hanh. (2006). *Teachings on Love.* Parallax Press, Berkeley, CA.

2 Dolinska, B. (1999). Empirical investigation into placebo effectiveness. *Irish Journal of Psychological Medicine,* 16(2): 57–58.

3 Mora, MS, Nestoriuc, Y and Rief, W. (2011). Lessons learned from placebo groups in antidepressant trials. *Philosophical Transactions B: Biological Sciences,* 366(1572): 1879–1888.

4 Kirsch, I, Deacon, BJ, Huedo-Medina, TB, Scoboria, A, Moore, TJ and Johnson BT. (2008). Initial severity and antidepressant benefits: a meta-analysis of data submitted to the Food and Drug Administration. *PLoS Medicine,* 5(2): 260–268.

5 Chopra, D. (1989). *Quantum Healing.* Bantam Books, New York.

6 Chopra, D. (1997). *The Path to Love.* Harmony, New York.

CHAPTER 10

Courage

Success is not final, failure is not fatal: it is the
courage to continue that counts.

Winston Churchill

What is courage?

Does it take more courage to start, to keep going,
or to stop?

Is there a difference between courage and
fearlessness?

Is courage conscious or unconscious?

Is courage good for us?

Is courage essential?

The Vikings might or might not have had a life instruction manual. Do you need to be told how to pillage, plunder and provoke? If the Vikings did have an instruction manual it might have been short, and it might have contained the only great Viking life wisdom tip that I know: *Die with your arrows in the front.*

If that needs more explanation I can add that apparently this was all you needed to do to get to Valhalla, the Viking warrior's heaven. All you need to do to get admitted to warrior's heaven, and not gate-crash worrier's hell, is die like a warrior — facing your enemy. If you die facing your enemy, then you have done your best and bravest. If you die with your arrows in your back, however, it means that you have done the opposite to your best and bravest: you haven't given yourself a proper life chance.

Note that in the Viking life manual there is no mention of results: it does not matter whether you win or lose, or live or die — only your intent matters. This is exactly the same principle as the one espoused in the great Vedic, Hindu, and increasingly universal life manual, *The Bhagavad Gita*: just do your best and your duty, and to hell with winning or losing.

Note also that according to the Viking life manual the way that you end your current life is the way you start your next one: in the paradise inhabited by those who did their best, or in another place. This is exactly the same as a Buddhist idea: if you can't manage to be your best at any other time in your life, then you can save your best for last — pull off something magnificent during your last breath!

What is courage?

Courage is knowing what not to fear.
Socrates as recorded by Plato

The Oxford online dictionary defines courage as 'the ability to do something that frightens one'. The great humourist and philosopher Mark Twain came up with a similar and earlier definition: 'Courage is resistance to fear, mastery of fear, not absence of fear.'

The Vikings had their own ideas about courage, and implied that it is indeed the absence of fear, as did others who have told us that fear can be transcended, even the fear of death, if we are courageous enough to transcend what we are fearful of losing. Hindus, Buddhists and American Indians, as well as Vikings, have made the point that to achieve peace of mind we need to recognize the inevitability of death, whether precipitated by arrows or whatever. To recognize the inevitability of death we need to recognize that everything passes, including human bodies, and also the arrows that can speed their passing progress.

Facing the circumstances of our lives — facing the music — can be like facing arrows, or worse. To keep facing, to keep learning, to keep laughing, to keep loving, to keep living, requires courage.

Whether 'tis nobler in the mind to suffer
The slings and arrows of outrageous fortune,
Or to take arms against a sea of troubles,
And by opposing end them?
William Shakespeare, Hamlet, Act 3, Scene 1

We don't have to be a Viking or even like Vikings, or watch them on television, to benefit from their life and death wisdom, just as we don't need to be, know or like great Danes to benefit from Hamlet's wisdom. We don't have to die to go to Valhalla. Our great life moment doesn't have to be our last moment; it can be our present moment.

The Wizard of Oz is another great fictional life manual, a thinly disguised

thesis on mind-fulness, heart-fulness and courage-fulness. In this classic children's and other humans' story, the disguised heroes tell the stories of each of us. The Scarecrow tells us the story of our lost mind-fulness. The Tin Man tells us the story of our lost heart-fulness. The Cowardly Lion tells us the story of our lost courage-fulness. Dorothy tells us the story of our lost home. We need courage to find our mindfulness and heartfulness, because we need courage to find our way home.

We don't need to be more scared than we need to be, because we can all be lions that have forgotten that we are lions, unaware of our true nature and true strength. The Cowardly Lion only thinks that he is a coward because he is scared of everything; however, he comes to learn that it takes great courage to realize that we don't need to be scared.

Types of courage

Courage doesn't always roar.
Sometimes courage is the quiet voice at the end of the day saying,
'I will try again tomorrow'.
Mary Anne Radmacher, Courage Doesn't Always Roar

John Fitzgerald Kennedy is famous for being an American president, and for being assassinated. Before he was elected American president in 1961, John Kennedy wrote, or actually co-wrote with his speechwriter Theodore Sorenson, a bestselling book called *Profiles in Courage*.[1] This book inspirationally describes the courage and integrity of some American senators who defied the opinions of their party and their constituents to do what they thought was right. Arthur Miller wrote a book called *The Crucible* about the Salem witch trials, which symbolized the lack of courage of some other modern-day American senators. They responded to Senator Joe McCarthy's communist witch hunts in the 1950s not by doing what they thought was right, but by doing what they thought was safe. If courage is doing what we think is right, no matter what, is that all it is?

Are there many forms of courage, or is there just one courage that manifests in different ways? Is the courage of a woman facing her second childbirth,

111

or of a soldier facing their second cavalry charge, the same courage? The second birth and cavalry charge is apparently more difficult to face than the first, because it means facing something that can be even scarier than the unknown: the known.

Is there a difference between the courage that allows us to face life without fear, and the courage that allows us to feel fear and to face it anyway? That great life teacher disguised as a fraud pretending to be a great life teacher, the Wizard of Oz, told the Cowardly Lion who wanted courage that he already had the courage that allowed him to do what he needed to do — in spite of his fear. When the Cowardly Lion, the Tin Man, the Scarecrow and Dorothy were faced with the terrible danger of the Kalidahs (wild beasts with heads like tigers and bodies like bears), the Cowardly Lion turned to Dorothy and said: 'We are lost, for they will surely tear us to pieces with their sharp claws. But stand close behind me, and I will fight them as long as I am alive.'

The Cowardly Lion told the Wizard that he didn't want that kind of courage, he wanted Viking courage: not being scared of anything. When the Wizard gave the lion this courage, by pretending to give it to him, and therefore allowing him to find it or create it himself, the lion indeed had no fear. Maybe, however, the Courageous Lion wasn't as loveable, or as human, as the Cowardly Lion.

Is it nobler in the mind to suffer the slings and arrows of *courageous* fortune, as well as Hamlet's outrageous fortune, by opposing and ending — or by enduring?

Certain cowardice or uncertain courage?

To every thing there is a season, and a time to every
purpose under the heaven. Ecclesiastes 3:1, King James Bible

Does it take more courage to stay or to go?

Does it take more courage to fight on or to give up?

Does it take more courage to win or to lose?

We make decisions all the time. Sometimes these decisions are big, or seem big, and sometimes they are small, or seem small. (What should I have for breakfast? Who should I have it with?)

Sometimes making decisions is easy, or seems to be, sometimes it's hard, or seems to be. Sometimes the decisions that we have to make are enormous and enormously hard, and the hardest thing about such decisions is that it seems as though we are making them alone. Courage is most valuable when it is most needed, and it is most needed when we have to make hard decisions. We often ignore the importance of hard decisions — ours and other peoples — but what good is courage if it doesn't allow us to face what needs to be faced?

Decisions can be hardest when they are least obvious, and this can be because there are compelling reasons to do something, and just as many compelling reasons to do something else. These are our dilemmas. Some diabolically difficult dilemmas include:

Do I live or die?

Do I help someone else live or die?

Do I stay or leave?

Being courageous doesn't mean being able to make the right decision: we often don't know whether our decision is right or wrong, now or ever. Being courageous means being able to make the *honest* decision.

Courage and heartfulness

Our deepest fear is not that we are inadequate.
Our deepest fear is that we are powerful beyond measure.
It is our light, not our darkness
That most frightens us.
Marianne Williamson, A Return to Love

It takes great courage to honestly face our life's adversities. It takes great courage to honestly face our fear. It takes even greater courage to honestly face our life. It takes our greatest courage to make our greatest decisions. It takes our greatest courage to live our greatest lives. It takes our greatest courage to face whatever is stopping us from opening our hearts and living as well as we can, together.

Being really courageous doesn't mean spending our life fighting. Being really courageous means spending our life loving.

> Was Jesus Christ more genuinely, honestly, heartfully
> courageous than Attila the Hun?
>
> Was Mother Teresa more genuinely, honestly, heartfully
> courageous than the Spanish inquisitors?
>
> Are you more genuinely, honestly, heartfully courageous
> when you decide to take or when you decide to give?

We don't know our greatest courage until we need it. We don't know our greatest courage until we feel it. We don't feel our greatest courage until we let go of our greatest fear. We don't let go of our greatest fear until we remember why we are alive.

Our greatest courage is our collective courage, our heartful courage. Our greatest courage comes from and flows to our collective heart — when we are courageous enough to realize that we don't need to fear life, because we are life.

The benefits of courage

> *Have the courage to follow your heart and intuition.*
> Steve Jobs

It takes courage to get out of bed. It takes courage to get out of the womb. It takes courage to get out of the tomb. It takes courage to die. It takes courage to live.

We will not make any mistakes if we don't do anything. We will not think or say or write anything unfortunate or ill-considered or inaccurate or inflammatory or wrong or dishonest or dangerous if we don't do or think or say or write anything.

Courage gives us no guarantee that what we will do will work out better than what we don't do. The only benefit of courage is that it gives us hope.

Courage in action

- Find the source of your courage.
- Feel your heart, no matter what it is doing.
- Listen to your heart, no matter what it is saying.
- Listen to your small and deep voice, until it dawns on you that what to do is as clear as the dawning day.
- Keep feeling your heart.
- Stay with your feeling for as long as it takes to forget time.
- Stay with your feeling for as long as it takes to feel the courage of realising that there is only one heart, only one heartfulness, only one ...
- See defeat as an opportunity for victory.
- See despair as an opportunity for hope.
- See contraction as an opportunity to expand.
- See adversity as an opportunity to love.
- See darkness as an opportunity to shine.

TAKE-HOME TIPS

- Don't think, do.
- Don't do, be.
- Just keep doing your best, for as long as you will then ... stop.
- Just keep going until you find ... stillness.

Examples of the courageous path to heartfulness

ANZAC COVE

Picture yourself on the first wave. You are on a boat, one of hundreds being rowed towards a dark shore. It is 3 a.m. and the moonlight has gone out. You are approaching uncertainty, maybe death by drowning or gunfire; maybe heroic immortality, maybe both. It is 25 April 1915 and you are entering destiny, via what will later be called Anzac Cove. Picture your sergeant telling you that there are times when it doesn't matter whether you live or die, just do, just do your best, and to hell with the reasons.

- What do you choose as the waves splash you to shore and the sounds of birds and shouting and bullets brings you to a distant earth?

- Do you choose despair or hope, or both?

- Do you choose fear or courage, or both?

- Do you become paralysed in your body and mind and heart by the myriad possible futures, or do you fall into a single, still-life eternity?

- Do you choose solitary sullenness or a shared silence?

- Do you find the courage to share a joke to help bring light to the deadly darkness?

- Do you find the courage to help when you could so easily hinder?

- Do you resent the other people you are landing with or against for being in your way, or do you realize that no matter what side of the boat or the bullets you are on you are on the same side?

- Do you find the courage to live or die, or both?

- Do you find the courage to win or lose, or both?

- Do you find the courage to do or not do, or both?

- Do you find the courage to give courage to those who you are facing your destiny with, even when you can't find it for yourself?

Picture yourself looking up at the first rays of morning light and it dawning on you that darkness is our opportunity to shine.

There are many wonderful examples of courage — other people's and our own — and of how it can speed us to and from heartfulness. There are also some wonderfully simple examples of courage, from real life and from not-quite-so-real life.

PERSONAL CRISES

Picture yourself waking up in any pre-dawn darkness and realising that you have to face an operation, or a speech, or a job interview, or a sick child, or a loved one who you didn't love enough yesterday, or a mistake, or another day without a job or a home or a reason to wake up, or so you think.

Picture yourself waking up to a wedding, or a funeral, or an accident, or hopelessness, or loneliness, or paralysis, or pain, or sickness, or doubt, or guilt, or a broken marriage, or a broken heart, or a broken life, or so you think.

- What do you do?

- What do you not do?

- Do you listen to your loud and superficial and false voice of fear or despair or selfishness, a voice that tells you to go on when something deeper tells you to stop, or that tells you to stop, when something deeper tells you to go on?

- Do you listen to your soft and deep and true voice that tells you to stop or go on, and why?

- Do you listen to fear or hate or love?

- Where do we find the courage to do and to be?

- What do we find when we look in and not out?

tHe von trapp famıLy's personaL crIsIs

On a lighter courageous note is the movie *The Sound of Music*, made in 1965, and based on the true story of the von Trapp family singers, written by Maria von Trapp and published in 1949. Adjusted for inflation, *The Sound of Music* is still one of biggest money-making movies of all time, and is a wonderful surprise for people who think that movies are never as good as the books or the reality they are based on.

The Sound of Music was the first movie I saw at a cinema, in Adelaide in about 1966, and I have seen it many times since. One of the wonderful memories and life lessons that this movie gave me was the power of courage. A great story of the power and beauty and necessity of courage was sung to me by a nun in the song 'Climb Every Mountain'. Now my four-year-old daughter, Miranda, also understands through a song story that there are times when we have to face leaving our monasteries or countries or wherever else we think is our home and realize that it lives in us, and through us, anywhere.

The nun sings 'Climb Every Mountain' to Maria (played by Julie Andrews), because Maria has fled back to the monastery she had left to be a governess for a retired naval captain and his seven children. She didn't flee from the von Traps because she was still scared of them; she fled because she was scared of her growing love for them. Maria thought that she had returned to the

monastery, where she was a not-highly-successful novice nun, because she wanted to live a quiet and spiritual life, devoid of children and naval captains. The head nun knew better: Maria was wimping out of her true heart's calling, self-actualisation or destiny, so she sang to Maria to inspire her to get back into her life ring and give her real life a real chance.

> *Climb every mountain,*
>
> *Ford every stream,*
>
> *Follow every rainbow,*
>
> *'Til you find your dream.*

The great Hindu/Vedic life manual *The Bhagavad Gita (Song of the Beloved)* gives us the same story as 'Climb Every Mountain' in *The Sound of Music* does — about 3000 years earlier.

PRINCE ARJUNA'S PERSONAL CRISIS

Prince Arjuna was like Maria, and all of us: meant to be doing something that he didn't want to do, or thought he didn't. Fortunately for all of us, Arjuna had the Hindu/Vedic universal equivalent of a Catholic nun to sing to him — the god Krishna, who symbolizes our deeper and braver selves. Arjuna's equivalent to be being sang to by a nun was being spoken to by Krishna, his charioteer. It takes Krishna 700 verses to inspire and convince Arjuna to get back into his life ring and overcome his real evil enemies and our symbolic ones in battle, whereas it only took Maria's nun six verses! The point of both of these stories is that we all need some help sometimes to find what we already know.

A link between *The Bhagavad Gita, The Sound of Music*, the Wimbledon tennis finals, and our own misplaced heartfulness is Rudyard Kipling's poem *If*.

If

Although Rudyard Kipling left India when he was six years old to go to school in England, it remained his home. Kipling was deeply influenced by Indian life and philosophy, including The Bhagavad Gita, which fuelled 'If', a poem written for his son, John:

If you can keep your head when all about you
Are losing theirs and blaming it on you,
If you can trust yourself when all men doubt you,
But make allowance for their doubting too;
If you can wait and not be tired by waiting,
Or, being lied about, don't deal in lies,
Or being hated, don't give way to hating,
And yet don't look too good, nor talk too wise;

If you can dream — and not make dreams your master;
If you can think — and not make thoughts your aim;
If you can meet with Triumph and Disaster
And treat those two impostors just the same;
If you can bear to hear the truth you've spoken
Twisted by knaves to make a trap for fools,
Or watch the things you gave your life to, broken,
And stoop and build 'em up with worn-out tools;

If you can make one heap of all your winnings
And risk it on one turn of pitch-and-toss,
And lose, and start again at your beginnings
And never breathe a word about your loss;
If you can force your heart and nerve and sinew
To serve your turn long after they are gone,
And so hold on when there is nothing in you
Except the Will which says to them: 'Hold on!'

If you can talk with crowds and keep your virtue,
Or walk with Kings — nor lose the common touch,
If neither foes nor loving friends can hurt you,
If all men count with you, but none too much;
If you can fill the unforgiving minute

With sixty seconds' worth of distance run,
Yours is the Earth and everything that's in it,
And — which is more — you'll be a Man, my son.

An even shorter version of 'If', *The Bhagavad Gita*, and *The Sound of Music*, is displayed at the players' entrance to Wimbledon's centre court arena, and they see it before they enter their fray:

> *If you can meet with Triumph and Disaster*
> *And treat those two impostors just the same ...*

Picture yourself facing a real or imaginary battle. Maybe it's located at Kurukshetra in northern India where Arjuna's battle was fought. Maybe it's in your office. Maybe it's in your car. Maybe it's in your kitchen. Picture yourself listening to a loud voice of despair telling you that you can't win, or to a loud voice of anger telling you that you must win. Picture yourself focusing on a voice so small that it is almost drowned out by your mind-made drama. Picture yourself listening to your small voice until it is a universal voice. Picture yourself doing all you ever need to do, or be ... your best.

The courageous bottomless line

Where is the last place that you would think to look for your courage that has gone missing in action? In your deepest fear. If we follow anything to its source we will find what we are really looking for, which is what we really need, because it is what we really are. It doesn't matter whether courage is feeling no fear, or feeling fear and doing or living anyway. Courage is our deep will when something or someone else says we won't. Courage is our deep will to start, to go on, and to stop — what needs to be started, gone on with and stopped. Courage is simply the will to allow life to live.

References and further reading

1   Fitzgerald, J. (1955). *Profiles in Courage*. Black Dog & Leventhal, New York.

CHAPTER 11

Knowledge

Where is the Life we have lost in living? Where is the wisdom we have lost in knowledge? Where is the knowledge we have lost in information?

TS Eliot, The Rock

We are one in knowledge.

Meister Eckhart

How are you?

Keeping busy?

What do you know?

What do you know? This was one of many once popular greetings and conversation-starters. As with many once-popular phenomena it is deeper than it seems, because if we knew what we knew we would be know-alls.

Namaste! This is still a popular greeting in some places, such as India and Nepal. It means 'The universal (divine) within me recognizes (knows) the universal within you.' This is really quite a magnificent greeting and conversation-starter, as are its many relatives, such as 'G'day, mate!' (God be with you, my friend!)

When we really recognize (know) other people, we really recognize (know) ourselves. When we really recognize (know) ourselves, we really recognize (know) other people.

Know thyself. This message was inscribed above the temple of Apollo in Delphi in ancient Greece, which was the place where a series of wise women known as the Delphi Oracle gave great practical life knowledge to people who needed it, and who knew they needed it. The people who visited the Delphi Oracle didn't really need to visit her, because deep down they already knew everything she would tell them, and because everything she would tell them was already in the message at the entrance. *Know thyself* wasn't and isn't a polite suggestion, or a self-help tip. *Know thyself* was and is a *commandment*. What we really need to know was never *out there*. Clarity begins at home, and always did. All true knowledge roads lead to home, even if they take detours to ancient Rome, ancient Greece, ancient and modern religions and philosophies, ancient and modern self-help books, and universities.

Real knowledge is real power. Real knowledge is about our real selves and our connections with other people's real selves. Being heartful means living as we know we can live, rather than living as we think we should live.

What is real knowledge, what is real?

To know, is to know that you know nothing. That is the meaning of true knowledge. Socrates as recounted by Plato

Is real knowledge knowing how to fix a tap, or fill out a tax return, or plant a wheat crop, or do sums without a calculator, or give someone a haircut that won't embarrass them or you, or win an argument, or not offend anyone, or seem sincere, or get elected; or is real knowledge deeper, and more deeply valuable?

The Oxford online dictionary reveals that knowledge is one our 1000 most frequently used words, and defines it as 'facts, information, and skills acquired through experience or education; the theoretical or practical understanding of a subject'.

What do you know now?

Plato recounts that Socrates gave us a deeper definition of knowledge: justified true belief. Johann Wolfgang von Goethe aims at the heart of knowledge, and at our heart, with 'All the knowledge I possess everyone else can acquire, but my heart is all my own.'   And then there is Jimi Hendrix: 'Knowledge speaks, wisdom listens.'

So what is real knowledge, and what is it for? Does real knowledge go in and out of fashion? Does real knowledge grow or change, or is it infinite and eternal because it means knowing the infinite and eternal?

Was the common knowledge that our planet is flat, and that the sun goes around it, and that we contemplated all that with a brain with about 4 billion nerve cells in it, and that our mental capacities can be read via the bumps on our skulls, real? Is the common knowledge that our internet and mobile phone connections make us more connected, and that mass media and other planetary pollutions and loss of community are small prices to pay for 'progress' real? Does one human knowledge size fit all of our human needs, or are there different kinds of knowledge? If there are different kinds of knowledge, which of them is real?

What do you know?

Knowledge types

> *Knowledge without justice ought to be called cunning rather than wisdom.*
> Socrates as quoted by Plato

We have knowledge that lives in our minds, and we have knowledge that lives deeper than our minds.

The symbol of our mind knowledge is fire, and our discovery of fire made us modern humans modern humans. With fire we could extend our living environments, such as by being able to live in colder places, and stay up late at night talking about the weather. With fire we could extend our planetary influence, such as by developing steam engines and internal combustion engines and nuclear power.

The ancient Greek myth of Prometheus wasn't a quaint old story about quaint old long-gone people and gods. Prometheus, like all myths and like all history, is alive now, and he can help us understand what is happening now — if we listen. Prometheus was a god who liked us humans so much that he decided to give us a gift that would make us like gods, for better or for worse. So he gave us the gift of fire, which symbolizes the power of our minds to transform — to know how to make cold hot and hot cold, and right wrong and wrong right.

The snake did the same thing for us or to us in the Garden of Eden — for better or for worse, for us or for it. The knowledge-tree snake seduced us into acquiring mind power, and it is our separate thoughts that separate us. For better or for worse we have been losing the innocence of our universal mind ever since. Psychologists describe this phenomenon as 'the theory of mind'. Until we are about 18 months old we don't 'know' that we are separate from other people, that we have separate minds. We 'progress' to this form of knowledge at about the same time that we develop language, which gives us the ability to describe and experience separation. Prometheus and the knowledge-tree snake are still with us, and they are still giving or selling us knowledge. Is it real?

There are lots of ways of dividing knowledge and everything else we know into types. Plato and Socrates divided knowledge into divine knowledge, which really just means knowledge of our true selves, and human knowledge, which really just means knowledge of all the stuff that distracts us from knowing our true selves. Plato and Socrates warned us about getting sucked into blatantly non-divine knowledge. They gave us a cave story through which we can see that addictions to televisions and computers and other virtual realities are an addiction to knowing the non-real thing rather than the real thing.

Philosophy's distant descendent, cognitive psychology, also gives us a choice between knowledge types. Episodic knowledge is personal knowledge, such as of what I had for breakfast and whether or not I liked it. Semantic

knowledge is impersonal, factual knowledge, such as of how good for me my breakfast was. A slightly less distant relative of philosophy is Gestalt psychology. This describes our ability to perceive and therefore create wholes (shapes) and not just the bits or bytes that make wholes. Gestalt psychologists demonstrated our ability to macro-perceive by giving people ambiguous pictures, which we can see, for example, as either an old woman, or a young woman with a scarf. A more modern proof of this remarkable human ability is when our computer tests us to see if we are really human by giving us numbers or letters in strange forms that we have never seen before. We humans can do what computers can't: recognize that it doesn't matter what form numbers or letters take, they still have their essence — we can perceive wholes.

We can link philosophy's distinction between human and divine knowledge and cognitive psychology's distinction between personal and impersonal knowledge, and Gestalt psychology's distinction between knowledge of parts and wholes, and even an unbranded distinction between knowledge of ghosts (spirit) and knowledge of machines (including human ones). All of these ways of knowing knowledge are ways of knowing the difference between what is real and eternal (the knower), and what is unreal and fleeting (the known).

We can know ourselves as a collection of body and mind bits and bytes, or we can know ourselves as a whole, something that is more than our body and mind bits and bytes. When we live at the personal knowledge level, we live second-hand lives, driven by ideas. When we live at the real knowledge level, we live eternally new lives, driven by experience.

How do we stop being modern cave men and women and live in light and delight?

Dead elephants don't jump

To keep doing the same thing and expect different results is insanity. Albert Einstein

What are you certain of?

The Oxford online dictionary defines 'certainty' as 'firm conviction that something is the case'.

> Is there anything beyond doubt, which can
> therefore free us from doubt?
>
> Is there anything beyond darkness, which can
> therefore free us from darkness?
>
> Is there anything beyond our mind, which can
> therefore free us from our mind?

George Bernard Shaw once told another great intellectual that there is only one word in English in which 'su' is pronounced as 'sh', and that is 'sugar'. The other great intellectual replied, 'Are you sure?'

You might think that you are sure that dead elephants don't jump, especially given that live ones don't (because they can't), but are you really certain of it?

> How does being certain help us?
>
> What's in it for me to know who I really am?

You might think that you are sure that the Earth moves around the sun, and that the Earth isn't flat, and that you have 100 billion rather than only 4 billion brain cells to think about that stuff with, yet would you be so sure if you were living in another time?

We can't really be certain of anything — even that this book is real or the hand that is holding it or the mind that is pondering it or the person who wrote it is real. All of this and everything else that we think is real might actually just be an illusion, a cosmic or comic mirage, a dramatic dream — *maya*. The only thing that we can really be certain of — the only thing that we can really know — is that we exist. We *know* that we exist, we know that 'I am', no matter what I think I am. Not even an omnipotent god or a snake can truthfully say we are not.

How to be a superhero

A man of knowledge lives by acting, not by thinking about acting.
Carlos Castaneda, Don Juan's Teachings

I am Cat Woman, hear me roar! Cat Woman

Superheroes are super guys and girls who regularly do super stuff, like fly through the air faster than a speeding thought train, and leap tall stories in a single bound. That's great, or so it seems, but is that all? The really interesting thing about superheroes is that they usually don't seem super all the time.

The nineteenth-century German philosopher Friedrich Nietzsche wrote some still well-remembered philosophical stuff such as 'God is dead'. This got him into a lot of trouble, because people didn't really know what it meant — then or now. He also published a book called *Superman* in 1885, which was once almost as famous as the *Superman* comic books that Jerry Siegel first wrote and Joe Shuster first drew in 1936, and which had influenced Siegel's comic creation.

Nietzsche's Superman got him into trouble when he was alive, and then got him and all of us into even more trouble when he wasn't, when, along with Wagner's operas, it inspired Adolf Hitler to believe that Aryans were an all-conquering Super Race. This comic-book interpretation of good and evil was actually the opposite of what Nietzsche meant. Real supermen and -women simply know who they really are and who we really are — a great and universal being — disguised as a small and fleeting human idea of a universal being.

Gautama realized that we are all a Buddha (one who is truly awake), not just him. Jesus realized that we are all a Christ (anointed, redeeming), not just him. When we realize who we really are, we are all superheroes.

How do we drop our disguise? It's not as hard as you think. Real power doesn't come from what you know; it comes from who you know. Real power comes from real knowledge, and real knowledge is of who we really are, and never what we think. We know who we really are when we let go of who we think we are. Real power comes from knowing that we are more than we think we are, and from knowing that we are connected to more than we think we are connected to.

Alan Watts was an English philosopher who moved to America and helped popularise Eastern life knowledge systems such as Buddhism and Taoism in the West. He produced many great public performances and books, including *Does It Do You, Or Do You Do It?*[1] and *The Book: On the Taboo Against Knowing Who You Really Are.*[2] In these performances and books, Watts put

out there what many of us might suspect *in here*: that formal life knowledge systems, such as religions and philosophies, can actually take more knowledge from us than they give us. It is not helpful to be told that you are bad, by whatever name, and that personifications of the divine, such as Jesus Christ and Gautama the Buddha, have a patent on perfection.

The messengers of organized religions and philosophies can lose their universal message in their own ideas about their messages, and they can lose the essence of what they are saying in how they are saying it. The true message that all life knowledge messengers are giving us is that we are all 'the truth, the whole truth, and nothing but the truth'.

When we remember to forget who we think we are, or who people tell us we are, we know who we really are.

Knowledge and heartfulness

The learning and knowledge that we have is, at the most, but little compared with that of which we are ignorant. Socrates, quoted by Plato

What do you know that is beyond knowing?

What do you know that is beyond power?

What do you know that is beyond your mind?

What do you know that is really true, and truly real?

What do you know when you have forgotten everything?

What do we know when you have lost everything?

When we know that we have nothing left to lose, we know everything: we know freedom, we know love, we know everything described and not described in this book, because we know our essence — our hearts and their connection with other hearts.

What we know in our hearts is real knowledge because it is the experience

of who we really are. Heartful knowledge doesn't have fashions or fads, it simply is. This isn't knowledge that we learn, it isn't even knowledge that we remember, it is knowledge that we are.

How do we get it? When Socrates said at his fatal trial that he knew nothing, he wasn't giving us an excuse, he was giving us his greatest secret. Knowing nothing in our minds means that we know everything in our hearts. Our minds know that we are separate — better than, worse than, more beautiful than, uglier than, richer than, poorer than. Our hearts know that we are connected, to each other and to our mutual source. The secret formula of life is:

The common denominator for all of us is

Life

When we open our hearts we know all, because being heartful gives us full access to life by giving us full access to love. When we are heartful we know all that we need to know, because we know that we are connected, and we know that we are beyond separation — we know that together we are one.

The benefits of knowledge

A human being is a part of the whole, called by us, 'Universe', a part limited in time and space. He experiences himself, his thoughts and feelings as something separated from the rest — a kind of optical delusion of his consciousness.
Albert Einstein, letter, 12 February 1950

True knowledge is true freedom. True knowledge is our natural antidote to our delusions, our ignorance, our suffering. True knowledge is our way out, and we will only find it when we go in. True knowledge is true life knowledge, and it will give us help, happiness and health, if we allow it to.

True knowledge operates at many levels, just as we do, and it benefits us at many levels:

- *The physiological level (body):* When we know what feels right with our bodies we know what feels wrong with them, and we know how to return to our natural state of balance and wellness. We can develop a good relationship with our bodies in the same way that we can develop a good relationship with anything or anyone — by really listening to them, really connecting with their needs, not ignoring them, not getting angry with them, or fearful of them; by responding to their subtle distress signals before they turn into blatant warnings. The key to connecting with our bodies is connecting with our bodily sensations, being fully aware of them, and fully accepting them, as they come, as they go, as they are.

- *The psychological level (mind):* When we know what feels right with our minds we know what feels wrong with them, and we know how to return to our natural state of balance and wellness. We can develop a good relationship with our minds in the same way that we can develop a good relationship with anything or anyone — by really listening to them, really connecting with their needs, not ignoring them, not getting angry with them or fearful of them, and responding to their subtle distress signals before they turn into blatant warnings. The key to connecting with our minds is connecting with our thoughts, being fully aware of them, and fully accepting them, as they come, as they go, as they are.

- *The life level (spirit):* When we know what feels right with our lives we know what feels wrong with them, and we know how to return to our natural state of balance and wellness. We can develop a good relationship with our lives in the same way that we can develop a good relationship with anything or anyone — by really listening to them, really connecting with their needs, not ignoring them, not getting angry with them, or fearful of them; by responding to their subtle distress signals before they turn into blatant warnings. The key to connecting with

our lives is connecting with the people who we share our lives with, being fully aware of them, and fully accepting them, as they come, and go, as they are.

Knowledge in action

- Know that there is more to us than meets our eye. We can experience life as we habitually and unconsciously do — blurred, personal, and problematic; or we can experience it as we can consciously do — clear, absolute and perfect. We can experience the waves at our surface, or we can experience the still ocean beneath them and including them. Submerge from knowing your surface self into knowing your deep self by connecting with what is beautiful and real and permanent, and by disconnecting with whatever seems to be anything else.

- Don't take life personally. Segue from thoughts of life to experiences of life by using the starting reality of pure knowledge, of your bodily sensations ... Without judgement or comment or resistance, allow yourself to be fully alive in the full connection of your mind, body, heart and essence, firstly by finding your feet ...

  - Move your awareness slowly and carefully through your body, from your feet to your head ...

  - Be aware of large and small sensations, and the flow of small and large energies, feeling and accepting all, as one ...

  - Spend enough time feeling your heart to feel its timelessness ...

  - Experience the eternal, the infinite and the immortal firstly as your bodily sensations that you begin to feel *impersonally, universally* ...

  - When your sensations don't feel like your sensations, your investment has returned.

- Come home. Return from whatever transitory life adventure you are on or think you are on to the stillness it started from. Our greatest knowledge is

knowing our way home ...

- **Allow the possibility that you are not who you think you are.**
- **Allow the possibility that you can change your life perspective as easily as you can change your mind.**
- **Allow the possibility that you are not a limited and personal being who occasionally has experiences of what lies beyond; you are what lies beyond, occasionally having experiences of limited and personal beings.**

TAKE-HOME TIPS

- Don't forget to remember to forget what you think you know. Live in and from what you really know.

- Know that it is not what you know, it is who you know. Really know yourself.

- Prioritize peace, not what causes you to lose contact with it.

- Don't react from what you think you know; respond from what you really know.

- Know nothing in everything.

- Open your mind and your heart until you know nothing, and therefore all.

- Don't just let the force be with you, *know* that you *are* the force.

Examples of the knowing path to heartfulness

There are plenty of public-domain life-knowledge dynamic databases that will give us the life answers we need if we give them the questions they need, and which will help us be superheroes.

The active ingredient of all public-domain life-knowledge databases — religions, philosophies, medicine, psychology, etc — is the most practical knowledge there is: how to replace our destructive ignorance with creative intelligence. How can we find and experience real life by living from what we know rather than from what we think we know?

Here are some public paths to true knowledge, to heartful knowledge, that live at the heart of our human help systems. These systems can take us a long way towards the light and delight of real life knowledge; however, they cannot take us all the way. Our final life solution lives in a place that no one else has the key to.

Ayurveda

The word '*Ayurveda*' means 'knowledge of life', and it describes an ancient Indian life knowledge system whose fringe benefits include physical, mental and spiritual health and happiness. According to this 4000-year-old universal philosophy/medicine, we can't be fully healthy or happy until we are free of what is really wrong with us: our ignorance of who we really are. When we really know our bodies and minds and how closely they are linked, and linked with other people's bodies and minds, we know our essence, our heart, our universally connected Self.

Ayurvedic and other ancient life/medical knowledge systems, such as traditional Chinese medicine, show us that health and happiness are our natural state, and that we can lose this natural state if we live unbalanced lives, spent living in *unnatural habitats* of destructive home, work, food and relationship environments. Living in an unnatural habitat is caused by unhealthy or unhappy thinking patterns, which are caused by our unhealthy or unhappy beliefs, such as that we are separate from each other, our true selves, or the universe. Unhealthy thinking patterns cause us to launch *mind missiles*, at ourselves and at other people. Mind missiles include thoughts like 'I will be happy when ...' and 'I am unhappy because you should have ...'

Modern mind–body medicine shows us the same thing that Ayurveda and other ancient life and medical knowledge systems show us, because they are linked — *we are linked*. We realize our whole life potential when we realize our whole and what makes us whole.

Some heartful living principles that we can extract from ancient and modern body–mind–life knowledge systems include the following:

- *Balance:* **Knowing what we really want and need helps us naturally balance our physical, mental and life diet, in**

our home, our work, our finances, our relationships and our whole lives.

- *What we do is done to us:* Whether we call this principle karma or justice or the price of freedom, we need to realize that we have to live with what we do to our bodies, to our minds, to our hearts, to other people's bodies, minds and hearts, and to our planet.

a Hard case study

A personal example of Ayurveda as a knowing path to heartfulness is my transition from researcher at the Victorian Transcultural Psychiatry Unit in Melbourne to Ayurevedic inpatient in India. I had health problems and life problems and wanted a way out, or in. As it happened, the World Health Organization sent us a research fellow all the way from Jaipur in the north of India. Dr Shrikrishna Kendal Sharma was the Deputy Director of the National Ayurvedic Institute in Jaipur, and his mission was to discover how Western psychiatric medicine could help Ayurveda's approach to mental illness. His short answer turned out to be 'by staying away from it!'. His long answer is another heartful story.

I persuaded a reluctant friend to join me on an Ayurvedic adventure, and Kylie and I ended up eventually in a hot, dusty and small Ayurvedic hospital in a hot, dusty and large town called Quillon, in India's deep south. The Amruthanjali Ayurvedic Hospital charged a dollar a night for accommodation and food, which seemed about right, plus the costs of the treatments. We did fifteen days of Ayurvedic hard time, which included physical and psychological treatments: various daily and twice-daily hot oil and spice bastings, massages, steamings, potions and, in my case, head shavings. The real treatment, however, consisted of our Ayurvedic doctor, Dr Pillai, regularly turning up unexpectedly in our hot and dusty ward and giving us real life lessons such as:

'There is cure for homesickness — when you go home!'

'You Westerners think thinking is the solution, but thinking is the problem!'

'The real cause of your bodily and mental problems is not what you think it is. The real cause of your problems is that you are ignorant of the little things, such as what to eat and how, and the big things, such as who you really are!'

We improved physically and mentally in response to our bastings, oilings, steamings and potions, as eventually we felt strangely healthy and our stress greatly lessened. Much more importantly, we discovered our lost heartfulness, which funnily enough began when we realized that we were suffering together, Kylie and I, and the billion or so Indians keeping us company, and the entire planet. We then realized that because we were suffering together there is something even greater that we can consciously do together: live together. When we realize that we are not suffering alone, we are not suffering.

I eventually went home and quit my job as a researcher at the Victorian Transcultural Psychiatry Unit, and restored old houses for a decade or so, which is another heartful story.

Buddhism

The word 'Buddha' translates from the language that Gotama the Buddha spoke, Pali, as 'one who is truly awake'. Buddhism is a philosophy/psychology/religion that originated in northern India about 2500 years ago, and what we think Buddhism is and what it really is are not necessarily the same thing, or no-thing. The gist of the Buddha's teaching, although not necessarily of Buddhism, is that we are all Buddhas — all enlightened — when we wake up to the truth of who we really are and are not. When Buddhism started being studied in the West in the nineteenth century, it was decided that it was 'nihilist' in that it says that we are not real, we are living in an illusion — *maya*. Buddhism actually says what all great life knowledge systems say, in its own

way, and that is that the self we think we are isn't ultimately real — our essence is beyond our individual form, and beyond any physical or mental form. Our realisation that there is more to us than meets the *me* is our way out, and in, and beyond.

Buddhism's primary living principles have been borrowed by many currents of mainstream medicine and psychology, and they have not always been acknowledged. Mindfulness, for example, has its origins in Buddhist meditation and other life practices, as well as in other life knowledge systems. Acceptance therapy (ACT) is a popular if often unacknowledged tributary of mindfulness. Cognitive behavioural therapy is based on an insight of Buddhism and other ancient life knowledge systems: our destructive emotional states are not caused by the events that we think cause them, they are caused by our mind's interpretations of these events.

Some heartful living principles that we can extract from the Buddhist life knowledge system are:

- *Acceptance:* **The positive power of accepting that we can't change what is, so the deeper our relationship with reality the deeper our happiness and health.**
- *Compassion ('loving kindness'):* **This can cure us of our ultimate life malady: forgetting that each so-called separate self is connected to its source and therefore to all tributaries of the common source.**
- *Transience:* **All things must pass — even our physical or psychological or spiritual malady that we only think is eternal.**

a Hard case study

A personal example of Buddhism as a knowing path to heartful knowledge is my experience of vipassana meditation. This apparently is the meditation technique that Gautama/ Gotama the Buddha used, and it is the key technique on which mindful and heartful meditation is based. *Vipassana* translates as 'to see things as they really are', and it can be

further translated as 'making friends with reality', or even 'realising our interconnectedness with all things'.

Vipassana is traditionally taught in a ten-day meditation retreat, during which you are not allowed to talk except to the person guiding the course, whom you can ask a brief question or two about the technique during daily half-hour individual question-and-answer sessions. I sat in a queue once for almost half an hour to ask a question, and I wasn't even sure what the question would be until it came out. It was: 'Is the Buddhist idea, or rather non-idea, of ultimate nothingness — no self, emptiness — actually exactly the same as the Vedic philosophical and Hindu religious non-idea of an absolute reality or Self?'

The vipassana guide was silent for a few moments before dramatically exclaiming: 'Yes!'

Taoism

The word 'Taoism' is pronounced 'dowism', and its meaning is even trickier to deal with properly because it doesn't have one. Taoism emerged in China at about the same time that Buddhism did, and is said to be untranslatable. Nonetheless, I will have a go and translate it as 'life'. The Tao is definitely not considered by Taoists to be a system of life knowledge or anything else, probably because it simply *is* life, rather than *knowledge about it*.

Some heartful living principles that we can extract from the Taoist life knowledge non-system are as follows:

- *Go with the flow:* **If we spend our lives floating downstream we will live a lot better and more enjoyably than if we spend our lives crashing along from disaster to calamity like storm-swept logs.**
- *Unity:* **Yin and Yang are the key Taoist symbol of our essential unity — everything contains its 'opposite'.**

Lao tzu's story

A personal example of Taoism as a knowing path to heartful knowledge is that of a founder of Taoism, Lao Tzu. When Mr Tzu was asked by a border guard to declare any valuables that he intended to take out of China (which he was leaving about 2500 years ago because it had become too hustling and bustling for him), he declared: 'Yes!' Lao Tzu then proceeded to tell the apparently highly patient (or receptive or bored) border guard the story which would become the great Taoist text, the *I Ching* (*The Book of Changes*).

Christianity

The word 'Christian' refers to a follower of Christ. The word 'Christ' comes from the language of the Bible, ancient Greek. The ancient Greek word *'Christós'* means 'anointed one', and it comes from the Hebrew word for 'Messiah', anointed by God. Christianity emerged approximately 2000 years ago from the older Judaic religion, with which it still shares a common text — the Old Testament. It could be said that Christianity was a necessary softening of its Judaic source, which is equivalent to Buddhism's softening of its Hindu source, quite possibly because humanity was growing up, and needed more loving guidance and less unquestioned authority. As with any great knowledge system, the central messages of Christianity can be very complicated and theoretical, and they can also be very simple and alive. As with any great knowledge system, Christianity is most powerful and most valuable as a gift rather than an order.

Some heartful living principles that we can extract from the Christian life knowledge system include the following:

- *The power of love:* Unlike the Bible's Old Testament, which gave us ten commandments, Jesus gave us only one: 'I give you a new commandment — to love one another. Just as I have loved you, you also are to Love one another.'
- *The power of hope:* Salvation is our eternal reason for hope. The permanent possibility of our being saved (from the

hell of our limited and limiting idea of ourselves) means that that no matter how bad things seem there is always a way home, to the heaven of our unlimited, real and eternal life.

father david's story

A personal example of Christianity as a knowing path to heartful knowledge is a short conversation that I had with an Anglican minister, a conversation which ended about 40 years after it started ...

When I was about eight my brother and I were trainee altar-boys in a very small church in a very small town called Sea Lake on the way to Nhil, at the end of nowhere. After much theological rumination, I told Father David that I didn't like the idea of a personal and external God. Father David told me to pull in my head, and soon I was an *ex*-trainee altar-boy. When I said the same thing to Father David about 40 years later at the successful altar-boy's fiftieth birthday party, Father David said that seeing God as an Absolute, Impersonal, All-encompassing Ultimate Reality is entirely valid: the Lord works in mysterious ways, whether you call him God, or Buddha, or the Absolute, or the Tao.

Philosophy

The word 'philosophy' comes from the Greek word '*philo*' (love) and the Latin word '*sophia*' (knowledge, wisdom). Wisdom is the most practical thing there is, even though philosophy these days is unfashionable. Hardly anyone realizes that we all want what philosophy and religion and psychology and mindfulness can give us — heartfulness — no matter what path to it we choose.

Philosophy has been around for as long as we have asked questions about our lives, which means that it has been around for as long as we have. While

philosophy is taught in universities and resides in lectures and books, it also lives in our hearts. Philosophy has spawned some extremely popular modern descendants, who rarely acknowledge their tribal elder. Philosophy has the same relationship with its modern descendants as the moon which emerged from the Earth, and with grown-up children who emerged from their family homes: they rarely mention their parents yet still orbit around them!

Psychology is the science of what philosophy is the art of: knowing ourselves, and therefore living as well as we can live.

Some heartful living principles that we can extract from the philosophical life knowledge system include the following:

- *The answer to the question 'Who am I?':* **The answer to this question is that the asker of the question, our mind, will never know the answer to its question, because such answers are always in the future, which is an illusion. The answer to the question 'Who am I?' is already known, by the knower of the question, the knower of the answer, the knower of all — the consciousness that is aware of all, because it *is* all.**

- *The benefits of knowing who we are:* **When we know who we are, we know that there is much more to our lives than suffering, because there is much more to life than *our* lives.**

Returning to our Natural Gravitational Orbit

A personal example of philosophy and also psychology as knowing paths to heartfulness is my outward journey with both to their inner destination. After many years of 'studying' and 'teaching' psychology and philosophy, I realized that there is actually nothing to either of them, or to anything else that I think I need to learn. Real knowledge arizes when we forget the system that took us out of the gravitational pull of our habitual ignorance, and launch ourselves into our universal heartfulness space.

The knowledge bottomless line

Where is the last place you would expect to find your lost knowledge? Is it your ignorance? Is it is your path out of your ignorance?

There are plenty of signposts pointing to our deep and deeply valuable life knowledge; however, there is only one deep and deeply valuable life knowledge that they are pointing to. There are plenty of places to look for knowledge, but there is only one place to find it.

During the zenith of the Roman Empire there was a popular saying, which was especially popular with Roman emperors: 'All roads lead to Rome.' When we lose our life signposts and find our life, we know that 'All roads lead to home.'

References and further reading

1   Watts, A. (2012). *Does It Do You or Do You Do It?* Audio CD.

2   Watts, A. (1966). *The Book: On the Taboo Against Knowing Who You Really Are.* Random House, New York.

3   Dawkins, R. (2003). *A Devil's Chaplain: Selected Essays.* Weidenfeld and Nicolson, London.

4   *King James Bible.* John, 13:34.

CHAPTER 12

Hope

We must accept finite disappointment,
but never lose infinite hope.

Martin Luther King, Jr

The human heart has hidden treasures,
In secret kept, in silence sealed —
The thoughts, the hopes, the dreams, the pleasures,
Whose charms were broken if revealed.

Charlotte Brontë, 'Evening Solace'

What do you have left when you have nothing left?

What do you have left when what worked yesterday
doesn't work today?

What do you have left when you need a higher dose
than you needed yesterday?

What do you have left when, despite what Christopher
Columbus and your science teacher and your
psychiatrist told you, your world is flat?

What do you have left when the person whom you loved
more than love, or life, or laughter, devoured your
heart, and still claimed to be a vegetarian?

What do you have left when your greatest life hero
turns bad and rants on television?

What do you have left when your foolproof gadget or
business partner or romantic partner admits that they
fooled you?

Hope has been around for a long time, maybe for even longer than its opposite. There are ancient descriptions of the power and purpose and practicality of many important things, and these are called myths. Myths have come to mean stories which aren't true, or are no longer true, such as the 'myth' that pasta is good for us, or even Thomas Szasz's provocative *The Myth of Mental Illness*. Myths are really about that which is deeply and essentially true — so true that it doesn't look true. The ancient Greeks had a myth about hope:

pandora's box

A young woman called Pandora was given a box by a disguised god and told not to open it. Giving someone a box and telling them not to open it is like giving a child a gift-wrapped present and telling them not to open it, or giving people a nice garden

with a nice apple tree in the middle of it and telling them not to eat the apples. If we understood the gods, however, we would be gods. Pandora opened the box, of course, and all the world's problems came barrelling out of it in a flash. This upset Pandora and her husband considerably, and then they noticed something at the bottom of the box which crawled out slowly and gracefully and magnificently, like a reluctant superhero — hope.

What is hope?

I find hope in the darkest of days, and focus in the brightest. I do not judge the universe. Dalai Lama

The Oxford online dictionary defines hope as 'a feeling of expectation and desire for a particular thing to happen'.

What really is hope?

Is hope real?

Is hope a myth?

Is hope good for us or bad for us?

Is hope hopeless?

Does hope take us to or from heartfulness?

Albert Camus was a French existentialist philosopher superstar who died at the age of 46 in a motor-bike crash in the year I was born. You might not think that a French existential philosopher can be a superstar, especially if you understand French existential philosophy (and congratulations if you do!). There was a time and a place, however, when you couldn't walk into a university or bar in Paris or New York without tripping over one.

French existentialist philosophers such as Jean-Paul Sartre and Simone de Beauvoir and Albert Camus told me things when I was an undergraduate student of philosophy, literature and psychology that I couldn't even hope to understand, or thought I couldn't. They even told me about the hopelessness of hope. Actually Plato and Blaise Pascal and others had already come up with similar ideas, and the medical and psychological research literature would later say that hope *can* be bad for us, as well as essentially good.

That false counsellor. Socrates, quoted by Plato

We never live but expect to live. We are never happy, because we are readying ourselves for our future happiness. Blaise Pascal, Pensées

Albert Camus was young and handsome and intelligent and adventurous, as well as being a Nobel Prize-winning writer and a great philosopher, and it's nice when our great creators are moderated by being human as well as being great creators. Camus claimed in his *Myth of Sisyphus* that hope was actually the worst thing to come out of Pandora's box, and I have been wondering about that from time to time ever since.

Maybe hope itself isn't hopeless. Hope has been described by our great human help systems as our most valuable human attribute, or consolation prize. Maybe what hope is, and whether it's a good or bad for us, depends on its *type*. Maybe hope can be our greatest harmer and our greatest helper.

Hopeless hope

Hope is a waking dream. Aristotle

We can explore how a particular kind of hope can take us to heartfulness, and how another kind of hope can take us away from it. Hopeless hope is recognized by a common term 'false hope', which shows the great perceptive power of the common. There is also the common term 'blind hope', which also recognizes hopeless hope. So how can we recognize the vital distinction between fool's hope and 24-carat genuine hope?

False hope

False hope comes from the constant vain desire of our small and separate and temporary self to grow into something large and connected and eternal. This is why we develop addictions and obsessions and grudges, because they are fuelled by our ego's great need to be more than it is and to have more than it has. Our ego — our individual self — can never achieve what it thinks it wants, because our egos are fuelled by the idea that they are separate from other egos. It doesn't matter how much we inflate our ego's idea of itself, it will always want more than it has, and hope for more than it has, because it wants what it isn't. If our egos got what they really wanted they wouldn't be egos anymore.

False hope means wanting what we think we can have, but actually can't have, or keep. We can want what we don't have so badly, and hope for it so hard, that we become obsessed. False hope is false because a false hoper doesn't realize that even if they get what they want they won't be happy, because it isn't what they really want.

False hope is why we take the bait.

Blind hope

Blind hope is hoping for something even when we don't really think we can have it — we hope anyway, not in a happy heartful way where we are connected to what we are hoping for, but in a dark, dour and delusional way. Some well-known individual examples of hopeless hope are unrequited/unrequired/unreturned romantic love, addictions which are fuelled or fooled by beliefs such as that the next horse or cigarette or drink or argument will be the winner, and plastic surgery. One well-known mass human hopeless hope is the fountain of youth.

the great white hope

Jack Johnson was a great black heavyweight boxer of the early twentieth century who finally became the world champion in 1906. This happened when a white champion, the Canadian

Tommy Burns, finally fought Jack Johnson, in Sydney. This manifestation of black power caused great consternation to many white people, who consequently embarked on a massive search for a white champion, and the contenders were known for many years as great white hopes. Adolf Hitler had a similar great Aryan sporting false hope in response to Jesse Owens's 1936 Berlin Olympics triumphs, and Captain Ahab had a false aquatic hope for the demise of a great white whale.

Hope and heartfulness

Everything that is done in this world is done with hope. Martin Luther

What do we really hope for?

Who really are we?

These questions are connected, because what we really want is what we really hope for, and this is connected to who we really are. We have a fundamental hope that is deeper than our hopeless hope — for what isn't and never will be, because it is always in the past or in the future. We really want to be connected with other people, and be happy in a way that lasts because it isn't related to or dependent on anything which won't last. Our deep human hope is to be who we really are, because when we are who we really are we are connected, happy and free, and we just are.

How, then, does hope take us to our natural state of heartfulness, or how does heartfulness take us to our natural state of hope? When we are heartful, we are fully present to our life gifts, and we are not wanting or hoping for something to happen in the future. When we are heartful, we don't experience hope as a gnawing idea that we don't have what we want, but as a life force. When we are heartful, we realize our deep hope because we realize our full life and connectedness.

We lose heart and heartfulness when our clear and complete awareness is clouded by thoughts, including false hopeful thoughts. When we let go of our thoughts we experience ourselves so deeply that we are living hope, rather than

hoping to live better. When we are heartful, we transcend false hope because we are connected to the heart of hope and the heart of life, which are one. The source of real hope is what is happening here and now, not something that might happen or might have happened.

Some individual examples of heartful hope — hope which connects us with the life and love essence of others and ourselves — are:

- **hoping to do our best**
- **hoping to be our best**
- **hoping for the best for somebody other than ourselves, and**
- **hoping for our world to be the best world it can be.**

Some mass examples of heartful hope are:

- **hoping for world peace**
- **hoping for a raising of human consciousness, and**
- **hoping for everyone to be happy, healthy and free — not just me or the members of my family, community, country, culture or cult.**

The benefits of hope

Hope is the pillar that holds up the world. Hope is the dream of a waking man. Pliny the Elder

Scientific research on the nature of hope increasingly demonstrates its vital contribution to our health and wellbeing.[1, 2] Our capacity to develop a sense of hope has been linked to a range of positive outcomes, including:

- **physical health**[3]
- **psychological health**[4.5.6]
- **ability to cope with a range of physical illnesses,**[7] **and**
- **self-confidence and self-worth.**[8]

The evidence strongly supports our need for hope to function optimally and fully as human beings — to be fully heartful. However, hope is not viewed universally as a straightforward elixir of life by scientists or philosophers.

The reason for this apparent discrepancy is that hope's supporters and detractors are not attacking or defending the same thing. It is actually hopeless hope that Camus, Sartre, Aristotle, Pascal, Nietzsche and other philosophers and scientists have denigrated. The scientific researchers Omer and Rosenbaum,[9] for example, saw hope as a false and naïve belief in a positive future which could never be delivered, leaving the hopers in a worse state than they would have been in if they had never hoped! This is true of false hope for the past or the future, but is not true of real hope, which is for what we already have, here and now.

Other scientific studies of hope have found a successful union of the 'theoretically and practically consistent' in 'hope therapy' and mindfulness practices in the relieving of distress and the improvement of coping in women with recurring cancer;[10] have found that 'narrative therapy' helps children with cancer and other life-threatening illnesses cope by moving their self-stories from despair to hope;[11] and found that hope and optimism are essential elements of psychiatric therapy.[12]

Hope in action

- **Don't get baited by false hope. If we didn't think we could get something with no strings attached, then we wouldn't get hooked — by anything!**

- **Honestly ask yourself who you are hoping for as well as what you are hoping for. Do you want something for yourself, to inflate your idea of yourself, or do you want it for a larger purpose? Practise hoping for something larger than your idea of yourself and what you want; a good place to start is by hoping for people other than yourself.**

- **Recognize the real reason for hope rather than inventing rationalized reasons. Real hope comes from our source, our essence, our heart. When we access the source of our hope we access the reason for it, and the reason for us.**

- Don't hope to be who you are not, to be someone with more of something you want or less of something you don't want. Don't hope to be or have anything other than what you already are and already have. Hope to realize that you don't need hope.

TAKE-HOME TIPS

- Hope to experience life rather than ideas about life.
- Open up to real hope, rather than contract to false or blind hopes.
- Recognize that while there is life there is hope, and while there is hope there is life.
- Recognize that you don't need a reason to hope.
- Hope from your heart, not from your mind.

Examples of the hopeful path to heartfulness

Billy Wilder directed a wonderful movie called *Some Like it Hot* that was made in 1959, starring Marilyn Monroe, Tony Curtis, Jack Lemmon and Joe E Brown. The ending was wonderfully hopeless, and wonderfully hopeful. For reasons essential to the ever-thickening plot, Jack Lemmon was dressed as a woman and was taken out to millionaire Joe E Brown's yacht in a small boat. Lemmon was masquerading as a woman and being dated by Joe E Brown so that his friend and jazz musician colleague Tony Curtis could entertain Marilyn Monroe on Brown's yacht. Things suddenly advanced further than anyone but the scriptwriter expected when Brown proposed to Lemmon, on the small boat. Lemmon protested vigorously and pointed out his many unworthinesses, which didn't bother Brown a bit. Eventually Lemmon abandoned all (false) hope of salvaging the situation and took off his disguise and confessed 'I'm a man!', to which Brown immortally replied: 'Nobody's perfect!'

Sometimes the only place to find invincible hope is in our hopelessness. There are many examples of hope dawning from hopelessness; you might even be able to think of your own … How about:

- What hope did a boy of African-American, Caucasian, American Indian and Chinese descent called Eldrick have of ever making a name for himself that people would want to remember? Eldrick 'Tiger' Woods is one of the most famous, richest and best golfers the world has known.

- What hope did a 46-year-old Scottish–Chilean non-writing English television executive called Erika Mitchell have of ending up a great book-writer, or rather a great book-seller? EL James has sold about 100 million book copies of an originally pay-on-demand erotica ebook, and seen it made into a hugely profitable movie.

- What hope did a nineteen-year-old girl have of winning a competition one dark night near a Swiss lake in 1816 to see who could come up with the spookiest story, when her competitors included the poets Lord Byron and (her future husband) Percy Shelley? Mary Shelley came up with a prize-winning spooky story and later novel called *Frankenstein*.

- What hope did an illiterate 17-year-old French peasant girl have of saving the world, or at least of saving France, or at least of saving France from English occupation? What chance did she have at 19 of being the youngest person to lead a major armed force, and do it successfully, and do it without any military training or background? What chance did Joan of Arc have of eventually being recognized and canonised as a saint?

- What hope did anyone have of breaking the unbreakable Second World War Nazi code called 'Enigma'? Alan Turing led the team breaking the hopelessly unbreakable code by fighting fire with fire. He developed a computer to understand a computer, and eventually to help us better understand our own computer — the human mind. Winston Churchill

described Alan Turing as the single person who contributed the most to the winning of the Second World War, and he did it without firing a shot. The Enigma symbolizes all of our hopelessly insoluble problems, and its code-breaking symbolizes the power of hope.

What hope do any of us have of solving our hopelessly insoluble problems, our own life enigmas? All of our unbreakable codes can be broken. All of our quests are for Holy Grails. All of our stories are stories of hope, and real hope is never hopeless.

persephone and hope

Scientific and philosophical characterisations of hope as valuable and realistic come together in the ancient Greek myth of Persephone, which provides a wonderfully modern example of hope. Persephone's despair and hope reconcile in an unexpected way when she eventually struck a bargain with her new husband, Hades, the King of the Underworld, who had taken her to his kingdom. Like many modern pragmatically hopeful couples, Persephone and Hades struck a bargain whereby she spent half the year above the ground, and half below it, which is why, incidentally, according to this myth we have winter.

It is always darkest before dawn. Proverb

The hope bottomless line

What do we have when we have nothing but hope? We have what we hope for.

References and further reading

1 Nolen-Hoeksema, S and Davis, CG. (2002). Positive responses to loss: perceiving benefits and growth. In CR Snyder and SJ Lopez (eds), *Handbook of Positive Psychology* (pp. 598–607). Oxford University Press, New York.

2 Tennen, H and Affleck, G. (2002). Benefit-finding and benefit reminding. In CR Snyder and SJ Lopez (eds), *Handbook of Positive Psychology* (pp. 548–597). Oxford University Press, New York.

3 Irving, LM, Snyder, CR and Crowson, JJ. (1998). Hope and the negotiation of cancer facts by college women. *Journal of Personality*, 66: 195–214.

4 Snyder, CR. (1996). To hope, to lose, and hope again. *Journal of Personal and Interpersonal Loss*, 1: 3–16.

5 Snyder, CR. (2000). *Handbook of Hope: Theory, Measures, and Applications*. Academic Press, London.

6 Snyder, CR. (2002). Hope theory: rainbows in the mind. *Psychological Inquiry*, 13: 249–275.

7 Barnum, DD, Snyder, CR, Rapoff, MA, Mani, MM and Thompson, R. (1998). Hope and social support in the psychological adjustment of pediatric burn survivors and matched controls. *Children's Health Care*, 27: 15–30.

8 Tennen, H and Affleck, G. (1999). Finding benefits in adversity. In CR Snyder (ed.), *Coping: The Psychology of What Works* (pp. 279–323). Oxford University Press, New York.

9 Omer, H and Rosenbaum, R. (1997). Diseases of hope and the work of despair. *Psychotherapy: Theory, Research, Practice, Training*, 34: 225–232.

10 Thornton, L, Cheavens, J, Heitzmann, C et al. (2014). Test of mindfulness and hope components in a psychological intervention for women with cancer recurrence. *Journal of Consulting and Clinical Psychology*, 82(6): 1087–1100.

11 Hedtke, L. (2014). Creating stories of hope: a narrative approach to illness, death and grief. *International Journal of Narrative Therapy and Community Work*. Issue 1: 1–10.

12. Kamaldeep, B. (2014). Hope and optimism must be at the heart of psychiatric practice. *The British Journal of Psychiatry*, 204(2): 170.

CHAPTER 13

Creativity

When you ask creative people how they did
something, they feel a little guilty because they didn't
really do it, they just saw something.

Steve Jobs

Creativity requires the courage to let go of certainties.

Erich Fromm

Are you a creator?

Are you a creation?

Are you both?

What are we when we create?

What are we?

In the beginning was the Word, and the Word was a lie, until someone believed it. We are all creators as well creations, and when we realize that we realize everything, because we realize that we create what happens, including what we would like to destroy.

Highly creative people, such as Steve Jobs and Wolfgang Amadeus Mozart, often say that they aren't creative because creativity happens through them: they don't do creativity, it does them. If creativity isn't something that we do, is it something that we are?

What is creativity?

There is nothing new under the sun. Ecclesiastes 1: 4–11

The Oxford online dictionary defines creativity as 'the use of imagination or original ideas to create something; inventiveness'.

Is that all there is to creativity?

Psychology defines creativity as a type of intelligence. Convergent intelligence allows us to converge on a single answer — to deduce, to work out by working in. Convergent intelligence contracts. Divergent intelligence allows us to diverge out to many answers — to create, to work out from our working out. Divergent intelligence is creative and it creatively expands. A classic item in a test of divergent intelligence is: How many uses can you think of for a brick? Would you like to give it a try?

Does your answer include using the brick
to drop on the toe of test-makers who ask too
many questions?

Is creative intelligence all there is to creativity?

Can we create other meanings for creativity?

Maybe our most creative answers to our most creative questions start with our realisation that there is nothing new and never can be, therefore nothing new can be created. Matter and energy are what they are, and although their forms change we can't make any more of them. And yet everything is new, because if there is only one moment then we haven't experienced anything before and will not experience it again. We can't really create anything because everything that already exists is all that there is, in varying patterns of matter and energy. What we create is really just a remembering of what we have forgotten, an uncovering of what we have covered up, and a revelation of what doesn't seem to be, yet.

The great movie-maker George Lucas was once asked how he could create so many wonderful new things, like wonderfully new monsters and robots and plots. He responded by saying that there is nothing new, he simply re-arranges what already is to make it seem new.

Creating our life story

The universe is made of stories, not atoms.
Muriel Rukeyser, The Speed of Darkness

Our good news story is that our natural state is happy, healthy and heartful. Our bad news story is that we can't create any of those things because we can't create anything that isn't already here. Our even better news story is that we *can* create happiness, health and heartfulness, simply by uncovering what we have covered. In the beginning was the revelation, of our creation.

157

Nietzsche Lives again

As we have learned, Friedrich Nietzsche was a nineteenth-century German philosopher who upset an amazing variety of people. This was mainly because the people whom he upset didn't really understand what he was saying, then or now, and therefore created negative mind-myths about him, rather than positive universal myths. Nietzsche offended Jewish people who thought he was pro-Nazi and anti-Jewish, because the Nazis adopted and misrepresented his *Superman* book's ideas. They didn't understanding that being 'super' doesn't mean 'being better than'.

Nietzsche offended Christian believers, and quite possibly many other theist religious believers, when he wrote 'God is dead!' In fact, Nietzsche was actually a passionate Christian who was unhappy that dogma and doctrine had stifled Christianity's life force. Maybe we can use the same logic to say: Philosophy is dead! Psychology is dead! Mindfulness is dead!

Nietzsche the creator

Nietzsche had something important to say about many things, and he had something particularly important to say about creativity: our second-hand thoughts can stick us in a mental history that stops us from creating new life.[1] This, therefore, stops us from being fully alive. Our personal history isn't what we think it is — our life story — it is really our lifeless story. The stuff that happens to us is Shakespeare's 'stuff that dreams are made on': it is our *play thing*, not our *real thing*.

Our real life story is the flowing river of our creative consciousness, which creates and observes our life events, not the stagnant pool reflections of who we think we are. When we get stuck in the mind-mud of what seems to be our lives we can create solutions, because we are solutions. If we are not fully creative we are not fully alive, and our natural life flow will be dammed by our second-hand questions, doubts and despondencies.

We are all great creative geniuses, potentially. We are all great storytellers, potentially. We are all great lovers of life, potentially. Creativity is our greatest power because it is our life power, and we can use it positively or negatively.

What are we creating when we tell ourselves and other people a story about our being chronically unsuccessful, or unhappy, or a victim, or sick, or unstable, or vulnerable? What are we creating when we tell ourselves and other people a story about our being chronically successful, or happy, or a victor, or never sick, or stable, or invulnerable? Whether they are good or bad, our stories are just stories, and our real power comes when we realize that we can't really create anything, because we already *are* everything.

Our mind-made creations are finite and fleeting. Who we really are is uncreated, infinite and permanent. Realising our infinite creative potential frees us to be who we really are and to really enjoy our life stories. We can allow ourselves a creative perspective shift, or scene change, by uncovering our mind-made life obstacles: our thoughts about our storybook life rather than our knowledge of our real life. Real creation — uncovering something deeper than our limitations and delusions — includes the power to heal a mind-made psychological or even physical sickness. Real creation includes the power to know that what feels good *is* good, and that what feels bad *is* bad. We can create an ability to love life and the people we share it with by uncovering our true connectedness with our shared essence.

Creating our life 'myth'

Man created God in his own image. Sigmund Freud

We don't see things as they are, we see them as we are.

One of the wonderful things about myths, and one of the wonderful things about life, is that there is more to them than what there seems to be. We can think about myths as we think about most things — too much. One of the things that we think too much about myths is that, like life, they are literal, and that they are superficial. That is like looking at an ocean and only seeing the

waves, or like looking at your life and only seeing your life drama.

Myths might seem like quaint and embarrassingly unscientific accounts of really important stuff such as the creation of our world. Australian Aboriginal myth, for example, includes accounts of the exploits of dreamtime deities such as an emu-footed sky-dweller. Greek myth, for another example, includes accounts of a large man holding up the world after which collections of maps of it are named.

Are myths scientific errors or creative wonders, telling us something deep and disguised and special about who we really are and therefore who we really can be? There can be a fine line between what we call myths and what we call religious belief systems' accounts of miraculous healing and divine knowledge revelation.

There are many creation myths, in many cultures. Maybe their real power is in their ability to help us create truth, by helping us uncover what seems to be getting in its way. Between them, Plato and Socrates described an even more ancient Greek creation myth. In this myth God doesn't create us and our world and our apps, because God is perfect, so anything God creates will be perfect. Where would be the imperfection in that, or the fun? According to this myth, God creates a Creator who is slightly imperfect, and therefore able and willing to create an imperfect world, such as ours. There is a similar Egyptian myth. The writings of the ancient Egyptian philosopher Hermes Trismegistus also reveal a Creator who created a Creator, maybe to avoid the cosmic or comic boredom of a perfect play.

Modern scriptwriters also avoid perfection (and clichés, like the plague!), because no one wants to watch a movie without surprises and unexpected things going wrong in it. No one wants a great novel without important problems to solve. JRR Tolkien created a land called Middle Earth and a book series about it called *The Lord of the Rings*. He called his creative process *sub-creation*, because he created or rather re-formed what had already been created. Maybe all of our great creative works are actually a great *re-creation*.

This raises some creative questions:

Why would anyone create an imperfect world?

Why would a cosmic creator create problems,
when it doesn't have to?

These questions are unanswerable, or at least unanswered. Maybe we can answer them by asking some other questions that are even closer to home:

Why would *I* create an imperfect environment?

Why would *I* create problems, for myself
and for other people?

Why do *I* make trouble?

Maybe we can answer these creative questions by looking at our big and small creative motives. Maybe our entire universe was created for us, or rather revealed to us, as a play — just for fun. Maybe the perfect being that perfected us, almost, deliberately made things challenging for us in the same way that a myth-maker and a scriptwriter deliberately make things challenging for their characters. Maybe this is all so that we can experience who we really are by finding out eventually who we are not. Maybe we make troubles for ourselves, such as arguments and anxieties, because we need such turmoils to make us feel fully alive, or to allow us to know what happiness really is by experiencing what it isn't. Maybe a perfect being created an imperfect creation in the same way that a myth-maker and a scriptwriter create their imperfect creations to experience itself through what appears to be something else.

If we are a hammer, or think we are, chances are everything we see will be a nail, or we will think it is. If we are a perfect universal being that *doesn't* realize that it is perfect, chances are that everything we see will be a problem. If we are a perfect universal being that *does* realize who it really is, at least occasionally, like an ugly duckling realising that it is a swan, chances are that we will see Heaven on Earth.

Maybe the world really is just a stage that we are going through, and the ultimate resolution of all of our life dramas is just enjoying the cosmic show. Maybe we don't enjoy the show and even develop anxiety, stress, depression and gloom about it when we don't see that we are actors, and we take the created parts of our uncreated whole too seriously. Maybe life is better than it looks.

Creativity and heartfulness

We are all in the gutter, but some of us are looking at the stars.
Oscar Wilde, Lady Windermere's Fan

If we don't like being stuck in the mind-mud of our usual way of looking at things, how can we get out of it? We can create heartfulness — full connection, peace and happiness — when we can uncover what is getting in its way. Do we need to read about how to do this, or wait until someone tells us how to do it, or can we find an answer ourselves, here and now, in the here and now? If we are too sick or tired or jaded or unhappy or anxious to *feel* heartfulness, can we *create* it? If we can't create anything, because everything is already here, how do we *uncover* our heartfulness?

Before we can right anything, we need to know what is wrong. Before we can create our solutions, we need to know our problems. Before we can lift our lives higher, we need to let go of our mental and emotional ballast.

If you are not as happy as you can be, not as fulfilled as you can be, not as connected as you can be, what is wrong? Are you a victim of your circumstances? Are you a victim of someone else's circumstances? Are you a victim? Please consider an even more creative possibility: what if you have created your problems? What if your problems are actually created in the problem factory that you think is a solution shop — your mind? What if your mind's problematic reactions to what you think is your life is actually worse than whatever you think caused your reactions? What if your only problem is that you have 'learned' somewhere that an open heart is as painful as an open mind and an open window, because it lets in rain as well as light?

Our only mind- and heart-made problem isn't that we learned how to close our mind and heart window, it is that we forgot that we closed it. Our great creative power is the cause of our deep life mess, whatever it is, that covers and disconnects our natural ability and inclination to live and love. Our great creative power is also our great cure. When we stop creating explanations and justifications and excuses and theories, we can start creating solutions, simply by taking off our bullet-proof and people-proof vests and letting our heartfulness flow …

When we are heartful, our heart is liquid, and is naturally giving, flowing and also resilient, because our life events will never scar or harden, they will merely ripple.

The benefits of creativity

Creativity is the power to connect the seemingly unconnected.
William Plomer

What if you feel stuck — in a relationship, or a job, or a mind malaise, or any uncomfortable condition?

How do you escape?

There is evidence that being creative helps us in our problem-solving and our solution generation. A study of successful Californian entrepreneurs, for example, showed that they tend to make their decisions by accumulating relevant information and then recognising that they know what to do at a deep level. Apparently their best decisions were made when they did what 'felt right'.[2]

A Dutch/American study[3] found that people with greater creative awareness are better able to solve *insight* problems than are people with less awareness. This benefit comes from going beyond Nietzsche's second-hand thinking patterns. Full awareness and acceptance frees our minds from their concepts — our ideas about what is. Full awareness and acceptance helps us realize the great potential of our non-conceptual mind capacities, such as our intuitions and our ability to creatively restructure 'problems'. An example would be converting stress mountains back to stress mole hills, and stress mole hills into mountains of positive life opportunity.

The authors of the above study didn't explore whether the deep and deeply connected awareness associated with heartfulness is more helpful than 'regular' awareness. There is a great opportunity for expanding research into the benefits of heartfulness, and also for expanding heartful research in general;

just as there was for mindfulness research a generation ago, and for meditation research two generations ago. The life-expanding potential of creative heartfulness research is as enormous as the life-expanding potential of creative heartfulness.

Creativity in action

- Take responsibility for your good and bad creations. Recognize that a lot of what you think was created by something or somebody else was actually created by *you*.

- Recognize that we can get stuck in good as well bad mind-mud. When we let go of anything that we think is all there is, or all that matters, we uncover great opportunities for removing our life limitations.

- Creatively allow a good resolution. This might be a new wedding vow, even many years after the first one, or it might be a work contract that your workplace and its lawyers don't even know about. Your resolution might be to stop damaging yourself or others by getting angry, or it might be to love people until they give you a real reason not to, rather than doing things the other way around. We can make a powerful all-purpose resolution by resolving to be the best person we can be, now.

- Try reacting to the next thing which you think has gone wrong in exactly the opposite way to how you usually do. Allow yourself to surprize other people and yourself, such as by smiling when someone does something you think deserves a frown, or worse. Allow yourself the creative satisfaction of fighting fire with love.

- In the beginning was the Word ... What word have you created in your heart? Is there a word so deep within you that no one can hear it, not even you, yet it influences everything that you do or say? Is this

word related to love or to fear? Is this word related
to no or to yes? If we creatively connect with our and
other people's heartfulness, we connect with what is
even deeper than our individual heart.

- Uncover your stillness. Find the missing link
between your problem life and your potential life.
Create your real solution. Act from stillness, not
from what is covering it up: the sticky stuff, the
ideas that you can't let go — thought, habits, trouble.
When we act from and rest in stillness all is well,
and we know it.

TAKE-HOME TIPS

- Allow creativity to arise and thrive in any path to or from
heartfulness.

- Don't worry about creating a good life; just uncover a good day,
starting by fully revealing and revelling in this moment.

- Don't worry about creating anything, just allow.

- Experience everything as if you are experiencing it for the
first time.

- Experiment with making heartfulness by faking it!

- Create stillness by uncovering it.

- Before revealing anything, ask if there is a need for it.

- Remember that we are puppeteers as well as puppets.

Examples of the creative path to heartfulness

A creative interview with a not-quite-living creative genius

mary shelley
(science/science fiction)

Interviewer: Today we have a very special great lover of life, and a creative genius appearing live, more or less, on *Life, what's in it for me?* You are a particularly interesting and inspirational creative genius, because like some ancient Greek and Egyptian gods you created a creator, who gave life to a creation ... You are also particularly interesting and inspirational because like Joan of Arc you were only nineteen years old when you started doing what made you famous.

You created a great literary and 'human' form, and you did it in a century when people didn't expect such things from a well-bred young lady — especially the type of creation and creator that you created.

Welcome back from beyond, and thank you for leaving the silent majority, at least for long enough to talk to us today. The creator of Victor Frankenstein, who was the creator of Frankenstein's 'monster' — Mary Shelley!

Mary Shelley: Thanks for having me on your show; I don't get to do many live radio interviews these days, for obvious reasons. I actually didn't do many when I was alive either, mainly because radios hadn't been invented!

Interviewer: So, Mary Shelley, author of *Frankenstein*, girlfriend and eventually wife of the poet Percy Shelley, what was it like as a woman (and a very young one!) to write a great novel about

topics that not many women wrote about or possibly even thought about in your era: science and horror?

Mary: I didn't think of myself as a woman writing a great work of science-inspired horror fiction. I didn't even think of myself as a woman, or of what I was writing as great anything, or of it being science-inspired or horror. Actually I just wrote, and what came out has been labelled all kinds of stuff by all kinds of people who think they know. A great story is great because it wasn't written as the creation of a particular person, from a particular time, of a particular gender ... A great story is just a great story. I believe that if you create attributes of a creator, whether the creator is God or a successful movie producer (and it seems as if there's not much difference!), then you cover up the creator's creativity. A creation is a creation regardless of its pedigree!

Interviewer: Let's ask you some really creative questions, such as why and how you wrote *Frankenstein*, and what was it like being with Percy Shelley. But firstly an introductory question so that we can establish a rapport, as recommended in the qualitative research chapter of Stephen's *Vital Statistics* textbook! ... Where do you go for holidays?

Mary: I can answer all three of your questions at once, because I am a creative genius, and because they are connected!

Interviewer: Terrific! Before you do that, however, I will provide some context. You started writing *Frankenstein* in the summer of 1816. This was soon after Napoleon's defeat at Waterloo, and Wellington's victory. There was a cloud of smoke caused by an enormous volcano which shrouded much of Europe. This was no ordinary summer!

Mary: And we were on no ordinary summer holiday! Percy and I and Lord Byron and his personal physician, Dr John Polidori, were on a holiday in Switzerland, staying at a lovely hotel by a lovely, if somewhat spooky, lake ...

We were just like a bunch of regular modern teenagers on a gap year, except that one of us was a lord, two of us were great poets, one of us was a soon-to-be great novelist, and one of us was a doctor. Poor Byron was broke and healthy most of his life, yet he still managed to employ a personal physician!

It was a dark and stormy night after a dark and stormy day and we decided to have a competition to see who could come up with the scariest story. We went to bed and I had a dream. The dream was the story of *Frankenstein,* which I told the next day. If I asked you to bet on which of two great poets, a personal physician, and the then-unknown 19-year-old girl would win the prize for the spookiest story, which of them would you choose?

Interviewer: Um, you?

Mary: No! Dr Polidori won the prize for the scariest story for his amazingly true-to-life account of the Loch Ness Monster's Swiss cousin, Bessie!

Interviewer: Can you tell me how and why *you* created a monster?

Mary: Can anyone? I was intrigued by the science of my time, by the discovery of electricity and by experiments conducted by scientists such as Galvani. A lifeless frog, for example, could be galvanized back to life, or so it seemed. This was a bit like your modern Michael Crichton, who took the genetic science of his day further than it had been taken to create *Jurassic Park* — I took the science of electricity further than it had been taken ... I allowed a creative force that was stronger than ordinary literary force to flow, and it led me to create an answer to the mystery of life. I wanted to know and then tell what it feels like to be a creator, and what it feels like to be a creation!

Interviewer: Why did your creator, Victor Frankenstein, create a flawed version of life, a 'monster' who did bad things and whose creator went a bit mad and chased it all over the world, to put a stop to it?

Mary: Have you ever created something you didn't mean to? Have you ever created trouble? Have you ever wondered why? Have you ever wondered why a creator would create a world full of imperfections? I didn't write *Frankenstein* to answer these questions, I wrote it to ask them!

From the radio show Life, what's in it for me? *94.7 The Pulse FM, 'Great lovers, of life' series.*

The creative bottomless line

Don't worry about anything. Don't even worry about worry. When we create our full creative living potential by uncovering it, there is nothing to worry about. No matter how far we think we have travelled from our heartful home we are always at home, and we always know this when we uncover it.

References and further reading

1   Nietzsche, F. (1957; originally published 1874). *On the Use and Abuse of History for Life* (A. Collins, trans.). MacMillan, New York.

2   Kabat-Zinn, J and Goleman, D. (2005). *Mindfulness @ Work: A Leading with Emotional Intelligence Conversation with Jon Kabat-Zinn.* (CD).

3   Ostafin, B and Kassman, K. (2012). Stepping out of history: mindfulness improves insight problem solving. *Consciousness and Cognition*, 21(2): 1031–1036.

part 3

new

heartful

HORIZONS

CHAPTER 14

Coming home to heartfulness

We shall not cease from exploration
And the end of all our exploring
Will be to arrive where we started
And know the place for the first time.

TS Eliot, 'Little Gidding'

It may be that the satisfaction I need depends on my
going away, so that when I've am gone and come back,
I'll find it at home. Rumi

Home is where the heart is. Pliny the Elder.

Would you like to know a secret?

Would you like to know the secret of life?

Would you like to know the secret of your life?

Would you like to dance with life, and not wrestle with it?

The secret of life, including your life, is ...

The secret of life is no secret.

The secret of life is freely available in the public domain.

The secret of life doesn't belong to anyone, else.

There is nothing to life, because life is life.

The secret of life isn't contained in any book, or theory, or explanation, or words. The secret of life lives in the heart of this book, and in the heart of any book or theory or explanation or words, and it lives in the heart of the reader of these words — you.

The secret of life lives in its livers: in our essential, eternal, immortal space, in our heart of hearts, in our mind of minds, in our essence of essences. The essence of our mindfulness lives in the space between our thoughts. The essence of our heartfulness lives in the space between our heart beats. The essence of our body lives in the space between our breaths. The essence of our solution lives in the space between our problems. The essence of me lives in you. The essence of you lives in me.

The secret of life lives deeper than in our life's circumstantial evidence, our life events. The secret of life lives in our *I witness* life evidence, our living experience which doesn't change, no matter what seems to be happening within its infinite time and space.

Living our lives fully, deeply, heartfully means living life from the inside out, and not from the outside in. We naturally discover this living secret when we let go of everything that we think about ourselves and *be* ourselves. When we choose to live in our real world and not in our mind-made virtual world, we allow what our minds would call a miracle: the realisation of our full living potential to be connected, joyous, vibrant, loving, fulfilled, at peace and free.

The secret of life is life.

The secret of heartfulness is heartfulness.

You don't need to understand heartfulness just as you don't need to understand life. Just allow yourself to really live. Just feel your kindness, or adversity, or humour, or contentment, or love, or courage, or knowledge, or hope, or creativity … until you feel its source.

We spend most of our life time looking out for something, because we spend most of our time living a filtered life in a time prison — our minds. We can get out of our cosmic jail free when we stop looking at its bars, and start experiencing the space between the bars.

A small story

I wrote some of this book while I was looking after my ailing father, Graham, when his wife, Rita, was having an operation. I was 'interrupted' by the sound of a siren. My father was equally vitally engaged at the time, reading a newspaper, and asked me to go out and discover the source of the siren. He was more aware than I was that sirens can mean that something important is happening, such as your house burning down. I went outside into the post-tropical wet-season cloudy morning, and soon saw flames and a fire truck. A neighbour's boat had gone up in flames.

Apparently Moses was once interrupted from his usual way of looking at things and thinking about things and feeling things by a burning bush. I had to make do with a burning boat …

My living vision didn't turn out to be an 'interruption' at all — to my life or my idea of it — or at least not the type that I thought it was. Our revelations are our interruptions, in disguise. Our problems are our opportunities, in disguise. Our ordeals are our adventures, in disguise. Our heartfulness is our heartlessness, in disguise. Our mind-made life is our real life, in disguise.

Nothing really matters, because nothing is all there is and all that matters. Our lives are a stage that we are going through — what better opportunity than this one to open our minds and our hearts and enjoy what we let out?

CHAPTER 15

Find your new heartfulness-opening potential

Great problems require great solutions.

Answer each of the following nine questions on a scale from
1 — Not at all, to **10 — Totally**

The more honest you are, the more valid the test.

1. How kind are you?

1   2   3   4   5   6   7   8   9   10

2. How well do you respond to adversity?

1   2   3   4   5   6   7   8   9   10

3. How good humoured are you?

1   2   3   4   5   6   7   8   9   10

4. How content are you?

1   2   3   4   5   6   7   8   9   10

5. How loving are you?

1   2   3   4   5   6   7   8   9   10

6. How courageous are you?

1   2   3   4   5   6   7   8   9   10

7. How knowledgeable are you?

1   2   3   4   5   6   7   8   9   10

8. How hopeful are you?

1   2   3   4   5   6   7   8   9   10

9. How creative are you?

1   2   3   4   5   6   7   8   9   10

Calculate Your Heartfulness-opening Potential

HOP Step 1: Add up the points out of 10 that you scored for each question.
HOP Step 2: Subtract your added-up score from 90.

The higher your HOP score, the greater your potential to open your heartfulness.

If your HOP score is lower than it was before you read this book, don't worry, it means that your heartfulness-opening potential has gone down because your heartfulness has gone up.

If your HOP score is higher than it was before you read this book, don't worry, it means that your heartfulness-opening potential has gone up.

If your HOP score is the same as it was before you read this book, don't worry, it means that whatever you are, you are it consistently!

CHAPTER 16

Some more heartfulness-opening resources

When you know the notes to sing,
You can sing most anything!

'Do-Re-Me', lyrics and music by R. Rodgers and O. Hammerstein,
The Sound of Music

Music

Modern music, as in anything composed after about 1750, can be distracting. Baroque and pre-Baroque music is often more heartfulness-helpful because it comes from a modern age when we were less distracted from our heartful source.

Books

> *The Bhagavad Gita*
> *The I Ching*
> *The Dharmapala*
> The collected works of Plato and Socrates
> *The Talmud*
> *The Bible*
> *The Quran*
> The collected works of William Shakespeare

Websites

> www.heartfulnessbooks.com

Practices

> Yoga
> T'ai chi
> Meditation
> Being in nature
> Volunteering
> Joining
> Working with love
> Living in love

Courses

> Vipassana meditation
>   www.dhamma.org
> The School of Practical Philosophy
>   www.practicalphilosopher.org/Worldwide

www.philosophyschool.com/Worldwide
www.schoolofphilosophy.org.au
www.practicalphilosophy.org.au
www.schooleconomicscience.org
The School of Life
www.theschooloflife.com

Heartfulness beats

Do unto others as you would wish others to do unto you. This is the meaning of the law of Moses and the teaching of the prophets. The New Testament, Matthew 7:12

Regard your neighbour's gain as your own gain, and your neighbour's loss as your own loss. I Ching, Chapter 49

Hurt not others in ways that you yourself would find hurtful. Udana-Varga 5:18

… and you should forgive and overlook: Do you not like God to forgive you? And Allah is The Merciful Forgiving. Quran, Surah 24, 'The Light', Verse 22

One should never do that to another which one regards as injurious to one's own self. This, in brief, is the rule of dharma. Other behaviour is due to selfish desires. Mahabharata, Section CXIII, Verse 8

Carry out a random act of kindness, with no expectation of reward, safe in the knowledge that one day someone might do the same for you. Princess Diana

I am content to follow to its source
Every event in action or in thought;
Measure the lot; forgive myself the lot!
When such as I cast out remorse
So great a sweetness flows into the breasts
We must laugh and we must sing,
We are blest by everything,
Everything we look upon is blest.
William Butler Yeats, 'A Dialogue of Self and Soul'

181

Dedication

To our fathers, including:

Stephen's — Graham
Gareth's — David
Benny's — Charlie
Anouska's — John